Free
For
Good

Free For Good

ERADICATE FEAR AND ANXIETY GOD'S WAY

MARIAN KING DROPS

Kravitz & Sons
INNOVATORS IN PUBLISHING, MARKETING AND ADVERTISING

Kravitz and Sons LLC
1301 Farmville Blvd, Suite 104
Greenville, NC 27834

Published by Kravitz and Sons LLC.

ISBN: 979-8-89639-100-5 (sc)
ISBN: 979-8-89639-099-2 (e)

Library of Congress Control Number: 2025903691

Whether you are a seasoned believer, or someone seeking a way out of the confusion, doubt, and fear you find yourself in, this book has something for you. Each chapter is grounded in truths from God's Word, providing the answers for the heavy burdens we struggle to carry and maintain. It is full of practical applications, with many examples of how the author has "walked-out" the truths she shares with the reader from her own personal experiences. "Free For Good" is not just a book about "managing" fear and anxiety in your life but will lead you on a journey to eradicating them for good.

I give this book 5 stars

- Mary Jane

Free For Good by Marian King Drops is my newest favorite book. I love the book cover showing a dove with the sun rays illuminating the bible. It provokes a warm and peaceful feeling.

This book is not hard to read, and it has a nice rhythm to it. The author invites you to come on a journey to discover that all your fears and anxiety can and will be eradicated when you put your trust in God. The chapters are separated into group categories: Come and See; Come and Know; Come and Follow; Come and Be Free.

__"Come and Know__ that fear is a common experience. What is uncommon is how God wants us to handle fear and grow from it." The author uses scripture to back up her statements and then illustrates with stories of her own experiences or stories from the bible. It is a comfort to me knowing that I am not the only one who has doubts and fears sometimes.

Each chapter ends with __Come and Pray.__ I love that. This gives me the opportunity to pray about what I just read. Her prayers are clear and concise. I have used a couple prayers personally, outside of this book reading.

When reading this book, I feel like I am taking information in. I then can contemplate and reflect on it, especially with the stories. Then bring it out to God in prayer.

I would highly recommend this book to anyone. Even if you are not experiencing fear or anxiety currently. It is a great book to keep on your shelf and re-read if you start going down that path. I plan on getting this book as a gift for people in my friend group.

- Heavenbound Girl

Free for Good by Marian Drops is a compelling read that stands out due to its deeply personal touch. Marian masterfully weaves her own experiences into the narrative, creating a relatable and engaging story that resonates with readers from all walks of life. Despite being centered on Christian themes, Marian's writing style ensures that it is not limited to a Christian audience. She has a wonderful way of drawing readers in, sparking curiosity about God's character, and encouraging them to seek a personal relationship with Christ.

- Frances

This book is chock full of insights and wisdom that feel like they came directly through Holy Spirit revelation. It was such a blessing to read and get to benefit from the author's deep understanding of important truths from scripture and how to apply them to overcoming your own fears, discouragement, doubts and other negativity you may be dealing with. Fresh new insights bring the verses alive in whole new ways you probably never thought of before. Overall I feel it is a very powerful book that is sure to encourage you, fill you with more understanding, and change your life for the better.

- Erin

Everyone -and I do mean everyone- needs this amazing book. Why everyone? Because at sometime or other everyone finds themselves in a position where they have no control over a situation they are in. That causes fear. A scary doctor report, a child at risk, not knowing where your next meal comes from, life savings lost in a downturn of the stock market, a job loss, a fear of not passing an important exam or certification, divorce, bullying, an unfounded accusation. Everyone goes through the scary times. Whether you believe in God or not, this book is for you. Why? Because when you're in a position that you have no control over, you need the only one in the universe who does have ultimate control and who just happens to completely know everything about you because He created you, He loves you dearly, and He wants to go through this hardship with you. This book is a tool to be used. It is a key that unlocks the fearfulness and anxiety, and opens the door to calmness, strength, and peace in knowing that you have the greatest, most loving power in all of the universe walking, hand-in-hand with you-guiding you, loving you, strengthening you, teaching you, fighting for you. How can that possibly be in this little easy to read book? That is what makes this book amazing and unique. Each little section identifies different areas that the reader may identify with at different times in his life. This author gives a brief but clear biblical foundation of God's ability in this particular area. God's words will tell you how He is there for you. Additionally, the author also reveals personal stories of her own scary times. This allows the reader to feel that they are not alone in facing scary situations. Others have experienced these things also. Additionally, it allows the reader to feel warm and welcome and willing to reflect on what fears or anxieties are affecting them currently. At a time when one can barely put a foot in front of the other to move forward in life, the author actually prays FOR YOU! The reader can take this prayer and recite it at any time to cry out to the Lord Jesus, to settle himself and put himself into the waiting hand of the Lord. Take this warm and welcoming tool and use it to connect you with a fierce, but loving God until you come out of this valley that you're currently in. Then be as His little child and continue to hold His hand to praise Him and rejoice with Him when you are through this hardship and enjoy the good things that He has for the you, the child He loves so very much.

- Lauren

Free for Good; Eradicate Fear and Anxiety God's Way by Marian King Drops Read it! Keep it handy to read often! As one who has experienced fear and anxiety off and on all my life, I would recommend this book to anyone who could say the same! This book will be a blessing and help to anyone who reads it! Because it is saturated with scripture and organized into 28 segments within 4 steps to freedom, the book could be used as a 28 day devotional. The prayers included in each of the segments will meet the reader personally and can be a springboard for further Spirit-led prayer as you personalize the prayer to fit your current circumstances. And as you meditate on and pray through the prayers, it's like having a prayer mentor by your side. The author's words in the beginning of the book really set the stage for her guided tour to victory over fear and anxiety. She invites *the reader to "Come and learn who Jesus really is. Let His words bring you spirit and life." Each of the 28 segments of the book will lift your eyes from your problems to His promises, His character, His everlasting love, His faithfulness, His compassion and much more. The author's stories give encouragement and comfort that you are not alone—you're not the only one struggling. And the stories of victory will fill you with hope and trust that God can work in your life too! The reader will find that this is a book to read and re-read often. Just get the book and see for yourself. Fern*

- Janet Otto (Five Stars)

I highly endorse Marian's book. The truths found in this book are life changing. Having struggled with fear and anxiety herself, she understands your pain. She provides you with Biblical answers and real life stories on how to be set free. Over and over you will be encouraged, strengthened and will feel yourself drawing closer to your Heavenly Father, loving him more and more. Want hope, victory, freedom? This book is for you.

- Fern

TABLE OF CONTENTS

Marian is a lover of Jesus, a wife, mother, grandma to the sons of her three "adopted Chinese daughters." She is a Bible teacher, graduate of Bible Study Fellowship, retreat leader, past board member of Moms in Prayer and of SEEDS San Diego. Marian has been a business and governmental consultant/trainer. Her missionary trips to 24 countries have given her firsthand knowledge of situations that strike fear into the hearts of people who struggle worldwide.

Marian starts her day with prayer, God's word, and a heavy dose of coffee. A well-worn verse from her Bible is 2 Timothy 1:7 NKJV

"For God has not given us a spirit of fear,

but of power and of love and of a sound mind."

Dedication

I dedicate this book to Jesus Christ who has loved me with an everlasting love and given me a love for the many others who are battling fear, anxiety, and depression.

Acknowledgment

First, I acknowledge my precious husband of 50 years, George J. Drops.

It is because of his loving, caring support that I was able to overcome fear, anxiety, and many other demons that assailed me in the early years of our marriage.

I am thankful for the patient, skillful efforts of our son David who designed the beautiful cover of this book and our son Jonny who helped in other ways to grant me time to write.

Thanks to Pastor Jurgen Matthesius and Pastor Jeff Rutkowski from Awaken Church for their messages that prompted me to take up this transcript that had lain dormant for nearly ten years.

Come

You are cordially invited to journey

through these chapters to discover

God's ways to eradicate fear and

anxiety from your life. Eradicate

means to tear up from the roots.

The Bible says, "Every plant that my

heavenly Father has not planted

will be pulled up by the roots."

Matthew 15:13

Introduction

Dear Reader,

First, I express my empathy that you are dealing with anxiety or one of its corollaries: fear, panic, depression, or obsessive worry. I am aware that such feelings/thoughts can be crippling. However, you do not need cliches, theories, or unrealistic platitudes. If you are like me, you want victory. You want freedom. You want to be able to breathe again. You want *life!*

You are probably wondering, "What does this person have to offer?" Has she experienced situations that cause loss of appetite, inability to breathe, trembling, and raw fear? My encounters with fear began at 8 when my hero died. A cerebral hemorrhage took Dad within a few hours. Mom and I moved back to our hometown of Cincinnati, Ohio, where we rented two rooms in a strange family's house. It was there that I became my mother's caregiver. Nine months later, I was orphaned when Mom died of cancer. A succession of frightening experiences followed: sexual abuse by an in-law, being sent to boarding school in another state, and abuse by one of the overseers at the school.

As I grew into adulthood, my approach to perceived dangers morphed from fearing to controlling them. The words of William Ernest Henley in his work Invictus became my battle cry.

"I am the master of my fate. I am the captain of my soul."

Perhaps this is an approach you have tried, possibly with a similar degree of failure. Control and fear are two sides of the same coin. But, giving up control has its own set of fears *unless* you yield control to the One who has ultimate control.

My "control" led to a place of suicidal desires, which only indicated that I no longer wanted to live in a place of bondage to fear and anxiety. Death seemed sweeter than anxiety and fear. Once I realized that my ways were leading to death, I took the chance of surrendering to the One who promised freedom and *life!* Gradually, I was able to face fearful situations without anxiety. If you want that same victory, give God a chance. Learn his path out of bondage and into freedom and *life!* Read *Free for Good.*

You will see many verses from the Bible in this book because the Bible contains truth. It is true whether you believe it or not. The Bible has stood victorious over decades of criticism. The French philosopher Voltaire once said, *"A hundred years from my death, the Bible will be a museum piece!"* One hundred years after his death, the French Bible Society set up its headquarters in Voltaire's old home in Paris. In spite of years of criticism of the Bible and its authenticity, it has remained true and its critics false. www.wayoflife.org

My book is divided into four sections: Come and See, Come and Know, Come and Follow, and Come and Be Free. Each section has seven chapters. Four and seven are numbers of completion in the Bible. I hope and pray that as you read this book, you will come to a place of completion in ending your bouts of fear and anxiety or, at the very least, learn how to defeat them should they reoccur.

When you read the Bible, it is not like reading any other book.

"God's word is alive and working. It is sharper than the sharpest sword and cuts all the way into us. It cuts deep to the place where the soul and the spirit are joined. God's word cuts to the center of our joints and our bones. It judges the thoughts and feelings in our hearts." (Hebrews 4:12 ERV)

No other written word does surgery in our hearts like the word of God. This is what Jesus said about His words,

"The Spirit gives life; the flesh counts for nothing. The words I have spoken to you—they are full of the Spirit and life." (John6:63b)

If you want to know the truth and be free, read God's words in this book and in the Bible. God's words cut at the root of your fear and anxiety. Please note that Bible references are from the New International Version unless otherwise marked.

There is a story in the Bible about a woman who had an issue of blood for twelve years. Basically, she had no control over her menstrual cycle. In Hebrew circles, this meant that she was an outcast. No one could associate with her or visit her in her home. If she accidentally touched someone, they would be considered unclean and need to perform a cleansing ritual. We are told in Mark 5:26, *"She had suffered a great deal under the care of many doctors and had spent all she had, yet instead of getting better she grew worse."*

Can you relate? You may have tried many treatments, formulas, drugs, and self-medicating to overcome fear and anxiety, only to find that you did not recover but only got worse!

This woman had heard about the healing powers of Jesus. She followed him in a huge crowd of people and dropped beside him so she could touch just the hem of his robe. Instantly she was healed. Instead of rebuking her for touching him, Jesus called her "daughter" and said that her faith had made her well. Come and learn who Jesus really is. Let His words bring you spirit and life. What do you have to lose? *Fear, anxiety, and depression.*

Come and See

Jesus looked around and saw them following.

"What do you want?" he asked them.

"Sir," they replied, "where do you live?"

"Come and see," he said. John 1:38-39a

*Therefore, many of the Jews who had come to visit Mary, and had **see**n what Jesus did, believed in him. John 11:45*

Come, see who Jesus really is.

The Role of Perfect Love

Come and see how perfect love deals with fear and its offspring.

"For the thing I greatly feared has come upon me, and what I dreaded has happened to me." (Job 3:25 NKJV)

People who are not even Bible scholars generally know the story of Job's trials. He was a man blessed with all sorts of riches that this world had to offer him. Yet, in the short span of one day, Job lost his animals, servants, children, and their house! Apparently, such disaster was something Job had spent considerable time greatly fearing. Such loss was something he had dreaded.

Left with his wife, Job did not receive comfort from her. Soon after, his health began to wane. He developed painful sores, possibly boils, from the soles of his feet to the top of his head. In response to his pain, Job's wife suggested,

"Are you still trying to maintain your integrity? Curse God and die!" (Job 2:9)

We can look at Job's circumstances and wonder if terrible things happened to him because he was a hardened sinner. However, scripture proves that was not the case by God's admission.

One day the members of the heavenly court came to present themselves before the Lord, and the Accuser, Satan, came with them.[7] *"Where have you come from?"* the Lord asked Satan. Satan answered the Lord, *"I have been patrolling the earth, watching everything that's going on."*

Then the Lord asked Satan,

"Have you noticed my servant, Job? He is the finest man in all the earth. He is blameless—a man of complete integrity. He fears God and stays away from evil." (Job 1:6-8 NLT)

The dialog continues with Satan asking permission to test Job to see if he will remain faithful to God amid trial. At this point, you may be wondering why we are examining such an old Bible story. What could it possibly have to do with our lives today? According to the wisest human who ever lived on the earth, King Solomon,

"What has been will be again, what has been done will be done again; there is nothing new under the sun." (Ecclesiastes 1:9)

So, if it was not Job's sin that brought on his many troubles, what was it? The opening scripture contains our answer. What he greatly feared and dreaded had come upon him. Fear can open a door for demonic activity. The story clearly states that Satan brought these trials onto Job. Anxiety, panic, a weakened immune system, a lack of confidence, and depression are just some of the consequences of fear in our lives. Many of these symptoms apparently plagued Job. You may recognize some that have been in your life as a result of the barrage of "bad news" that constantly assails our senses.

Fear is sometimes referred to as:

False

Evidence

Appearing

Real

This explanation of fear has deception written all over it. Lying is another word for deception. Jesus had something to say to the religious leaders of his day about deception and lies.

"You belong to your father, the devil, and you want to carry out your Father's desires. He was a murderer from the beginning, not holding to the truth, for there is no truth in him. When he lies, he speaks his native language, for he is a liar and the father of lies." (John 8:44)

Therefore, if fear is false evidence appearing real and deception comes from the devil or Satan, the father of lies, then no wonder we read in 2 Timothy 1:7 *NKJV*, *"For God has not given us a spirit of fear, but of power and of love and of a sound mind."* The spirit of fear has not come from God, but from the deceiver. Therefore, it is a spirit that must be cast out. According to 1 John 4:8, *"There is no fear in love; but perfect love casts out fear because fear involves torment. But he who fears has not been made perfect in love."*

We are living in times that release a spirit of fear. Think of the stories that invade your living room via cable or streaming devices. What continually pops up on your cell phone? We constantly hear about disasters, new illnesses, and deaths. It seems normal to embrace fear and anxiety, but we just read that fear involves torment, and perfect love is what casts it out of our minds and hearts.

Practical steps to take in this exorcism can be found in Philippians 4:6-7, Phillips translation *"Don't worry over anything whatever; tell God every detail of your needs in earnest and thankful prayer, and the peace of God which transcends human understanding, will keep constant guard over your hearts and minds as they rest in Christ Jesus."*

These verses are stated in a more contemporary version in the Message Bible,

"Don't fret or worry. Instead of worrying, pray. Let petitions and praises shape your worries into prayers, letting God know your concerns. Before you know it, a sense of God's wholeness, everything coming together for good, will come and settle you down. It is wonderful what happens when Christ displaces worry at the center of your life."

Therefore, if you make decisions based on what you fear, recognize that a spirit is directing your choices, not the Spirit of the living God! Another spirit sometimes directs what is taking place in our lives. The Bible describes it as a spirit of heaviness. Have you felt it, like a weight upon your whole being, taking you deeper and deeper into depression? Isaiah 61:3 reveals how the Spirit of the Sovereign Lord will come to "bestow a garment of praise instead of a spirit of heaviness or despair.

There is a story in the Bible where King Saul was plagued with a spirit of heaviness. To dispel that spirit, the shepherd boy David was brought in to play his harp. David is the author of most of the psalms in the Bible. When he played his harp, praises were offered to the Sovereign Lord and Saul's spirit of heaviness had to leave. He became calm again. The resource page at the end of this book contains a list of praise songs to get you started in dispelling the spirit of depression, when and if it plagues you.

COME AND PRAY

Heavenly Father,

I come to you on behalf of these readers. You are telling them in these verses to bring their anxious thoughts to you. You already know what they are, but you want these troubled ones to tell you precisely what they need from you. Thank you that you hear. You have probably helped this one in the past, sometimes in ways, s/he was not even aware of. Teach these readers to cast out fear by depending on your unconditional love to bring your Peace into their minds and hearts. Thank you, Lord, that You invite us to cast **all** our anxiety on You because You care for us. (1 Peter 5:7)

Fear Of the Lord

Come and see that fear of the Lord is the hatred of evil and the beginning of wisdom. It overcomes all other fears.

Moses said to the people,

"Do not fear; for God has come to test you, and that the fear of God will be with you to keep you from sinning." Exodus 20:20

The people have just witnessed the evidence that God Himself has visited Moses on Mt. Sinai. They have heard thunder and a trumpet; they have seen lightning and smoke, causing them to tremble with fear.

According to my recollection, there was only one time I trembled with fear. It was an example of what the Bible says in Isaiah 66:2,

"Has not my hand made all these things, and so they came into being?" declares the LORD. "These are the ones I look on with favor: those who are humble and contrite in spirit, and who tremble at my word."

It was a time in my life when God was confronting me with a need to look inward. Usually, I tend to be an active, task-oriented person, busy and often in a hurry. That kind of lifestyle is perfect for masking internal issues. However, my life had come to a point where those problems needed to be addressed, and God was showing me that.

Feelings of abandonment from my childhood loomed over me like a dark cloud. I hadn't even realized that I had established an emotional wall intended to keep out hurtful feelings. Brick by brick was sealed with the emotional mortar of fear, rejection, pain, and bitterness.

As that wall grew higher, something was happening beyond my notice. Yes, I was proficient at keeping out bad feelings, but good, nurturing, supportive, loving, and caring feelings were blocked as well.

The God who said I am made fearfully and wonderfully was not satisfied to watch me bury myself behind such an indiscriminate wall. As I became aware of the need to tear down the very source of security I had so *carefully* constructed, I looked to God for help.

In faithfulness, He led me to two women from my church, a psychologist and a homeschool mom, and to the book Inside Out by Larry Crabb.

As the battering ram of obedience tore down that *"protective"* wall, what I found behind it was a trembling nine-year-old girl whose world had disintegrated with the death of her parents. She needed help to find her way out of the rubble and into the integral adult life to which her responsibilities were calling her.

My amazing friends and even Larry Crabb, through his insightful book, were acting much like Moses in this scene. He addressed his trembling followers as a father would treat a frightened child, *"Do not be afraid."* Next, he explained:

1. What God is doing – *testing you!*
2. So that the fear of God will be with you
3. To what end? To keep you from *sinning*

Let us look at the phrase *"fear of God"* more closely. It may seem like a contradiction when Moses says,

"Don't be afraid…God is giving you fear of Him."

To understand God's meaning in the Bible, we need to look at the language He speaks, which in this case is Hebrew. The word for fear (yirah) means reverence, evoked by the demonstration of God's mighty acts. If we stand in awe of the might and power of our God, we are more likely to obey Him. Just as a child who has a healthy fear of his Father's headship will keep his Father's rules.

Dear one,

Is God testing you in your present circumstances?

If you are His child, He has only one purpose: to conform you to the image of the sinless Christ. (See Romans 8:28-29) Know that He is acting out of love, just as He was in my life.

In reference to the very incident in Exodus 20, the author of Hebrews warns in 12:25-29,

"See to it that you do not refuse Him who speaks. If they did not escape when they refused him who warned them on earth, how much less will we, if we turn away from him who warns us from heaven?

At that time his voice shook the earth, but now he has promised, "Once more I will shake not only the earth but also the heavens."

The words "once more" indicate the removing of what can be shaken—that is, created things—so that what cannot be shaken may remain.

Therefore, since we are receiving a kingdom that cannot be shaken, let us be thankful, and so worship God acceptably with reverence and awe, for our "God is a consuming fire."

COME AND PRAY

God,

Your power scares me but also intrigues me. I am amazed that one so powerful is also compassionate. Help me understand the role of repentance and what it really is because I see that you will consume any sin I bring to your altar of repentance. Reveal any walls I have created to *protect* myself from your interference. Help me understand that those same walls are keeping out your guidance, your perfect plans, your protection, and provision. Teach me proper fear of You so that I might not sin against You.

Fear Of Man: A Snare

Come and see that fear of what others think of you is a trap.

"Fear of man will prove to be a snare, but whoever trusts in the LORD is kept safe." (Proverbs 29:25)

This verse caused me to investigate what a snare truly is.

"A snare is one of the simplest traps and is very effective. It is easy to produce and to set in large numbers. A snare traps the animal around the neck or the body. It consists of a noose made usually by wire or a strong string."

WikiHow states that snares should be placed in an area the prey frequents. They can be used in any weather, or in the day or night.

What exactly is the fear of man? One definition describes it this way – 'a pattern of inordinate desire for the approval of others, which affects every area of life, from personal choices to feelings about one's value and purpose.'

Fear of man is a snare or trap that can affect my life and all the places I frequent. It can affect me during the day or the night. It manifests in the following ways: as a need for approval/fear of disapproval, criticism, and humiliation; a need for acceptance, honor, and recognition. We can recognize it by second-guessing our decisions, being timid when we should be bold, disobeying God, and judging our self-worth by what others say about us. As you read these definitions, do you feel a noose tightening around your neck?

The proverbs verse presents us with a clear choice: find my value, acceptance, and affirmation in God or seek to find it in people. I spent far too much of my life making the latter choice, seeking to please others, wondering what they thought of me, and fearing their displeasure or rejection. The vast majority of such thoughts revolved around me. Once I yielded my life to the only One who could save and redeem me, I sensed His unconditional love and acceptance. As Jesus increased in my thoughts and emotions, 'I' decreased. Self-focus gave way to His all-encompassing love. My attention, thoughts, and desires turned more to the needs of others.

So, in what way was the fear of man a snare? How did it ensnare me?

1. The "bait" was other people's acceptance of me. Since I frequently sought that acceptance, it was easy for the enemy of my soul to snare me with frowns, critical words, rejection, and outright opposition.

2. Once trapped, I would fall into discouragement, doubt, and despair. Those feelings would lead to resentment, bitterness, and hostility if not corrected.

The way I learned to deal with this snare of fear of man was through a program called 'Jesus Ministry.' In this program, there is a segment that deals with spiritual strongholds. We are told in 2 Corinthians 10:4,

"The weapons we fight with are not the weapons of the world. On the contrary, they have divine power to demolish strongholds."

A stronghold, in this passage, means the arguments and reasonings by which the disputant endeavors to fortify his opinion and defend it against his opponent. Once trapped, we build a fortress around our choices and constantly retrofit its walls, thus erecting a spiritual stronghold.

In the 'Jesus Ministry,' the participants were given a set of questions to determine if a particular stronghold plagued them (e.g., anger, pride, love of the world, fear of man, unbelief.) It is amazing how many times a person would say, "I don't think I have that stronghold," but after answering the questions, they recognized that this was, indeed, their stronghold.

Once a stronghold is discerned, it is brought down through a three-step process called the 4 R's.

1. **Repent** – Fear of man is often the result of wounds or injustices from our past. Though the wounds were not our fault, we have established sinful patterns. We may need to confess the sin of self-absorption or of not believing God's words about us were true. In repenting, you may need to confess to caring more about the opinions of others than the words and commands of God.

2. **Receive** – Thank God that you are fully accepted through the blood of Jesus. He promises that when you confess your sins, He is faithful and will forgive and cleanse you of all wrongdoing (1John 1:9). Now that you have confessed, you may receive God's forgiveness and cleansing.

3. **Resist** – Resist Satan and his demons, who have assaulted your mind with lies about who you are and how others or God feel about you. Renounce these lies and command Satan to flee. (Note that this step and the next one can only be accomplished by someone who has fully surrendered to Jesus and is born again.)

4. **Replace** – Replace fear of man with confident assurance in the love of Christ. Replace self-doubt with the truth that you are a chosen vessel, the beloved of Christ. Replace self-pity with the joy of being called and empowered to do kingdom work for the King of kings.

Fear of man is intended to enslave you, but Jesus Christ has set you free. In Him, you can have victory over the fearful thoughts that have been like a noose around your neck.

"It is for freedom that Christ has set us free. Stand firm, then, and do not let yourselves be burdened again by a yoke of slavery."
(Galatians 5:1)

By his death and resurrection, Jesus Christ has made freedom available to all. The following chapters will explain how we can access that freedom.

COME AND PRAY

Precious Jesus, I agree with the psalmist in 33:20-21,

"Our inner selves wait (earnestly) for the Lord. He is our Help and our Shield. For in Him does our heart rejoice because we have trusted (relied on and been confident) in his holy name."

Holy God, as this dear reader meditates on Your unconditional, relentless love, may their heart be filled with the acceptance of that love that drives away the fear of man.

The Lord, The Great I Am

Come and see that the great, the mighty Lord, is everything you need in the present moment.

"Only do not rebel against the LORD. And do not be afraid of the people of the land, because we will devour them. Their protection is gone, but the LORD is with us. Do not be afraid of them."
(Numbers 14:9)

The verse mentioned above is a fantastic plea on the part of Joshua and Caleb. They have just returned from scouting the land God provided for His people, the Jews. He brought them from Mt. Horeb to Kadesh Barnea in mere eleven days. (Deut.1:2; *It takes eleven days to go from Horeb to Kadesh Barnea by the Mount Seir road.)* This is the land promised by God to His people, a land flowing with milk and honey, a beautiful land. The scouts have found all of this to be true, and then some!

Their report to Moses testifies,

"We entered the land you sent us to explore, and it is indeed a bountiful country—a land flowing with milk and honey. Here is the kind of fruit it produces. But the people living there are powerful, and their towns are large and fortified. We even saw giants there, the descendants of Anak!" (Numbers 13:27-28, NLT)

How many times have you been precisely where God placed you, according to His promise, but all you could see were problems? I've often said that I have the gift of suspicion, which is not a gift at all. It's simply the ability to look at something so beautiful and suspect that it will turn out to be disastrous. The bottom line, it's a lack of trust in the promise and the Promise Keeper.

I found myself in this exact situation as a young bride. I had not surrendered my life to Jesus; I lived as I darn well pleased. And, unsurprisingly, it usually was not pretty. Of course, I did not yet know how to discern how God was directing me appropriately. Nevertheless, we married and began to share everything, including our sinful lifestyles. We both were pretty much unaffected by the way we were living. We were living the unexamined life that the philosopher Socrates said is not worth living. Our early marital existence contained little to no joy because we were utterly selfish, living for ourselves and our interests.

For my part, I could only see the faults of my new spouse. His many admirable traits were hidden in the background like a type of bas-relief. I was like the scouts in this story. Because my husband had left his life work to marry me, the marketplace offered only untested areas for him, causing fear for my security to loom in my heart like a Goliath. I certainly did not know the Lord like David in the Psalms.

In the case of the scouts spying out the Promised Land, the Anakim were indeed frightful. But they were no surprise to God. This was a tribe of giants (think Goliath.) God had already destroyed the mighty Pharaoh, chariots, and horsemen on behalf of His people, the Jews. Joshua and Caleb declared out of faith in their almighty God, "…we will swallow them up. Their protection is gone, but the Lord is with us."

It is amazing how fear can keep us from hearing the very words of truth and life. Because Joshua and Caleb had an intimate relationship with their God, they communicated His perspective on the situation. "The LORD is *with* us." LORD is our translation of Jehovah, the name God revealed to Moses in the burning bush – the great I AM. Yet, despite speaking truthfully, the people could not receive their words because of fear.

The name Jehovah designates God's nature as He stands in relation to man, as the only almighty, genuine, personal, holy Being, a spirit, and the Father of Spirits. (Smith's Bible Dictionary, p. 284)

That relatively insignificant preposition "with" is the Hebrew word 'eth,' meaning nearness and for. This Jehovah, this LORD God, this Almighty God is not only near His people; He is *for* them. David knew this LORD when he wrote in Psalm 27:1,

"The Lord is my light and my salvation—whom shall, I fear? The Lord is the stronghold of my life—of whom shall I be afraid?"

Anyone aiming to understand the God of David should read Psalm 27.

Choosing to fear man instead of trusting the Lord is an act of rebellion, a sin. We can feel fear, yet still consciously choose to trust the Lord. Are you facing some giants in your life today (divorce, debt, job loss, abuse)? Know that the very fact that you are reading this book is because God himself has directed you to see him, to know him, and to follow him. Even though you may not have fully surrendered to him, even though you may just be learning of your sin, he is with you; he is *for* you.

COME AND PRAY

Let's pray David's prayers:

Hear my cry, O God;
listen to my prayer.
²From the ends of the earth I call to you,
I call as my heart grows faint;
lead me to the rock that is higher than I. Psalm 61:1-2
For in the day of trouble
he will keep me safe in his dwelling;
he will hide me in the shelter of his sacred tent
and set me high upon a rock. Psalm 27:5

God,

I want you to be **for** me. I need your protection. Give me understanding of who you truly are.

God's Right Hand

Come and see that God's strong right hand can be your strength in the face of trials and tribulations. "*When you go to war against your enemy and see horses and chariots and soldiers far outnumbering you, do not recoil in fear of them; GOD, your God, who brought you up out of Egypt is with you. When the battle is about to begin, let the priest come forward and speak to the troops. He will say, "Attention, Israel. In a few minutes you are going to do battle with your enemies. Do not waver in resolve. Do not fear. Do not hesitate. Do not panic. GOD, your God, is right there with you, fighting with you against your enemies, fighting to win.*" (Deuteronomy 20:1 MSG)

Throughout each day, we face battles of one kind or another. Our enemies are the world, the flesh, and the devil – formidable foes. Each has a strategy to take us down, whether by overt or covert means. In fact, Satan is centered on coming to steal (our joy), kill (the very life of Christ within us), and destroy (our destiny). (John 10:10) The distractions of our world are crafted to keep us from being still. Busyness, frenetic activity, cares are devices that crowd out the possibility of knowing God through reading, meditating on, and memorizing His Word.

Speaking of these distractions, Jesus said,

1. *"worldly cares, the lure of riches, and the desire for other things come in and choke the word, and it bears no fruit."* (Mark 4:19) "*In the world you will endure suffering. But take courage! I have overcome the world.*" (John 16:33b)

2. *"I say then: "Walk in the Spirit, and you shall not fulfill the lust of the flesh."* (Galatians 5:16)

3. *"He who sins is of the devil, for the devil has sinned from the beginning. For this purpose, the Son of God was manifested, that He might destroy the works of the devil."* (1 John 3:8)

Jesus has defeated all three of our enemies and He has given us the instructions on how we can live in His victory. Just as the Jews' victory could be found in God's presence with them in Deuteronomy 20:1, so our victory is found in Jesus Christ who has overcome the world, who has destroyed the works of the devil, and who has given us victory over our own fleshly desires through His Holy Spirit. No matter what enemy you are facing today, know that God is ready to face that enemy with you if you only seek His help. And, God is ready to fight to win against your enemies.

He encourages us with these words from Isaiah 41:10, *"Fear not, for I am* with you; Be not dismayed, for I *am* your God. I will strengthen you, *yes, I will help you, I will uphold you with My righteous right hand."*

At first glance, this seems like a statement we can take for granted and gloss over. Not a good idea! Instead of glossing over these powerful words, let us look instead at the power of God's righteous right hand.

"Your right hand, O Lord, has become glorious in power; Your right hand, O Lord, has dashed the enemy in pieces." (Exodus 15:6)

"Show Your marvelous lovingkindness by Your right hand, O You who save those who trust in You from those who rise up against them." (Psalm 17:7)

"You will show me the path of life; in Your presence is fullness of joy; At Your right hand are pleasures forevermore." (Psalm 16:11)

"Your hand will find all Your enemies; Your right hand will find those who hate You." (Psalm 21:8)

"Your right hand has held me up; Your gentleness has made me great." (Psalm 18:35b)

"My soul follows close behind You; Your right hand upholds me." (Psalm 63:8)

"If I take the wings of the morning, and dwell in the uttermost parts of the sea, even there Your hand shall lead me, and Your right hand shall hold me." (Psalm 139:9-10)

"The right hand of the LORD is exalted; the right hand of the LORD does valiantly." (Song of Solomon 2:6 NKJV)
The LORD said to my Lord, *"Sit at My right hand, till I make Your enemies Your footstool."* (Matthew 22:4)

Dear reader, what enemies are you facing today, enemies that have convinced you they are more powerful, who have intimidated you into submission? Consider the words Moses spoke to the Jews in our beginning scripture.

"In a few minutes you're going to do battle with your enemies. Don't waver in resolve. Don't fear. Don't hesitate. Don't panic. GOD, your God, is right there with you, fighting with you against your enemies, fighting to win."

God is the same yesterday, today, and forever. He is no respecter of persons. He is calling you to remain resolute, unwavering. NO fear, NO hesitation, NO panic! Why? Because God is with you, fighting with you against your enemies, fighting to WIN!

COME AND PRAY

God, these words are encouraging. I want to believe that they are for me. I've struggled so long and hard to overcome the enemy of _____.

No matter what I do, I fall back into the same habits. I admit that my faith is weak. Please strengthen my faith; help me to believe that these words are true – that You really are fighting with me against my enemies. I give You my unbelief and doubt. Please replace it with the faith and trust in You that I need.

Do Not Be Discouraged

Come and see that every human being faces times of discouragement. In these trying times, it is important to remember that trust in God's faithfulness can restore courage.

*"Have I not commanded you? Be strong and courageous. Do not be afraid; do not be discouraged, for the L*ORD *your God will be with you wherever you go." (Joshua 1:9)*

The prefix-dis means: not, opposite of, deprive of, remove. (Web.) Apparently, the leader, Joshua, who had been such a bold, courageous follower of God in Numbers, ch.14, now appears to be deprived of courage. It seems that all courage has been removed from him after forty years of witnessing the rebellion and disobedience of the former Jewish slaves whom God set free from tyranny in Egypt. Forty years prior, Joshua was the faith champion, rallying the troops to trust in God's faithfulness. Now he is the one in need of rallying.

How can we know that Joshua's faith has waned? In Deuteronomy 31:7-8 as Moses is transferring leadership of the Jews to Joshua, he exhorts him:

*"Then Moses summoned Joshua and said to him in the presence of all Israel, "Be strong and courageous, for you must go with this people into the land that the L*ORD *swore to their ancestors to give them, and you must divide it among them as their inheritance. ⁸ The L*ORD *himself goes before you and will be with you; he will never leave you nor forsake you. Do not be afraid; do not be discouraged."*

In the same vein, when God talks with Joshua in chapter 1, he adds in v.7,

"Be strong and very courageous. Be careful to obey all the law my servant Moses gave you; do not turn from it to the right or to the left, that you may be successful wherever you go."

God knows the discouragement that is in Joshua's heart. He is about to lose his friend and mentor. The burden that Moses has carried for forty long years is about to be placed on his shoulders. The long-awaited promise of entering the promised land was on the cusp of being fulfilled, yet there are traces of fear is in his heart. Even when Joshua finally gives marching orders to his fighting men, they respond with a pledge of obedience to him with one last volley of exhortation,

"Only be strong and courageous." (1:18)

Have you, like Joshua, had faith in something? Perhaps it was a promise you read in the Bible or maybe a prayer you had earnestly prayed for, or a dream you felt God had placed in your heart. You have waited and longed for it, and through dark moments of uncertainty, you have felt that perhaps it wasn't meant for you. As King Solomon tells us in the book of Proverbs 13:12, *"Hope deferred makes the heart sick, but a longing fulfilled is a tree of life."*

I have been in this place more than once, but the time that stands out was during my oldest son's young adult years. David had become a follower of Jesus at five years old. Because he loved God's word and studied with me, his faith grew and blossomed wonderfully. It was not until his high school years that he met friends who did not share his faith. They introduced him to the ways of the world and he willingly participated.

These were fine young men, and were loyal family members and good students. They were simply at a place in their lives when they were exploring all the options that the world had to offer. The realm of the natural seemed far more appealing than matters of the spirit.

At that time, I clung to many promises from God's word, probably a book's worth. Praying friends from Moms in Prayer joined me in prayer. Like Moses, like Joshua's troops, like God Himself, they were my encouragers. My husband and I prayed God's word daily for David.

A verse that was a bedrock for me was from Proverbs 22:6,

"Train up a child in the way he should go, even when he is old, he will not depart from it."

We experienced a 13-year roller-coaster ride with David as he came to learn that a sinful lifestyle does not provide lasting satisfaction.

I was encouraged with this truth when I read Hebrews 11:25 which speaks of such a time in Moses' life. Surely in Pharaoh's palace he had enjoyed manifold worldly enjoyment. Yet, he came to a place, as did our son, which is described in this beautiful verse,

"He chose being mistreated along with God's people rather than enjoying the passing pleasures of sin."

While David has not experienced mistreatment among God's people, he has learned of the passing pleasures of sin and the need to forsake them and now joyfully serves in the children's ministry at his local church.

Dear reader, have you been waiting a long time to see the fulfillment of something for which you have been believing God?

You had strong faith in God's promises at one time, but now, as the fulfillment has escaped you for these many months, or perhaps years, you have lost your courage to believe that God's promise is for you.

If you find yourself in such a situation, I urge you to take courage from the following words Hebrews 10:35-36,

"So do not throw away your confidence; it will be richly rewarded.[36] You need to persevere so that when you have done the will of God, you will receive what he has promised."

Keep praying. Keep trusting. Keep declaring God's word over and over for that which you are hoping. As Joshua was dying, he spoke these parting words to his people,

"Now I am about to go the way of all the earth. You know with all your heart and soul that not one of all the good promises the LORD your God gave you has failed. Every promise has been fulfilled; not one has failed." (Joshua 23:14)

COME AND PRAY

Lord God, your promises are true because you are not a man that you should lie. You know what is inside my heart (job/financial need, desire for a baby, relationship, healing, greater love for You). You are a God who inclines Your ear to hear our prayers. I trust in You to bring the fulfillment in Your way and Your timing. I believe in You. Help my unbelief, dear Lord. Help me stay true.

The Shepherd's Provision

Come and see how God shepherds us as sheep who often go astray.

"Even though I walk through the valley of the shadow of death, I will fear no evil, for you are with me. Your rod and your staff, they comfort me." (Psalm 23:4 EHV)

Come and meet the shepherd of Psalm 23. While this Psalm is the work of David, the shepherd boy, it reveals many truths about our shepherd, Jesus.

The psalmist is walking *through* this valley. Sometimes our trials seem endless, with no sign of letting up. But we will pass through, based on God's words to us in 1 Corinthians 10:13 EHV,

"No testing has overtaken you except routine testing. But God is faithful. He will not allow you to be tested beyond your ability, but when he tests you, he will also bring about the outcome that you are able to bear it."

This world is a valley of the *shadow* of death. It does not represent real death for the one whose shepherd is the Lord! For He has said,

"I am the resurrection and the life. The one who believes in me will live, even though they die; and whoever lives by believing in me will never die. Do you believe this?" (John 11:25-26)

This is the true reason for fear to be gone and eradicated. Until now, the shepherd referred to in the third person (<u>He</u> leads me; <u>He</u> makes me) has suddenly been addressed in the second person. David says, "<u>YOU </u>are with me," designating a fellowship, a unity between the shepherd and himself.

This represents the very heart of Jesus, expressed in John 17:24, when Jesus prays to His Father for those of us who will come to know Him in our day and beyond.

"Father, I want those You have given Me to be with Me where I am...."

These words express the essence of Jesus' name Emmanuel – God with us. Friend, whatever valley you find yourself in today (sickness, abandonment, betrayal, false charges, loss of a friend), Emmanuel is committed to being with you in your trial. And, as He accompanies you, He is refining your faith to be like pure gold. (1 Peter 1:6-7)

Think of the last phrase in the verse mentioned at the start of this chapter, "Your rod and Your staff, they comfort me."

Did you ever consider the shepherd's rod and staff to be instruments of comfort? When a sheep strays, the staff is used like a choke collar to pull him back on the path. The temporary pain to the neck is meant to remind the animal to stay where he belongs. The rod, on the other hand, inflicts even greater pain. It is used to beat off attackers such as wolves or mountain lions to protect the sheep. But, when a sheep continues to stray, endangering the whole flock by drawing the shepherd away to find him, the shepherd will use the rod to break his legs.

Like so many forms of discipline that parents exact upon children, this one costs the shepherd as much or more than the afflicted sheep. Now the shepherd must dress his wounds each day and carry him on his shoulders to each new grazing area. The shepherd hopes his loving care and nearness to hear his voice will correct the sheep's troublesome behavior. Can you relate? Has God given you many chances to change? Think of these words and how they express God's heart, like the shepherd's, toward you,

"God has been kind to you. He has been very patient, waiting for you to change. But you think nothing of his kindness. Maybe you do not understand that God is kind to you so that you will decide to change your lives." (Romans 2:4 ERV)

Seeing that the rod and staff inflict intentional pain, how does David see them as a source of comfort? David realized that all humans have a tendency to stray. He could relate to this tendency in his sheep because he found it in himself. Just as he would not allow his sheep to continue to stray, our shepherd will not allow that either – for our sake and those we influence. David seemed to know by faith what the author of Hebrews would write thousands of years later.

"My son, do not regard the Lord's discipline lightly and do not become weary of his correction. For the Lord disciplines the one whom he loves, and he corrects every son he accepts."
(Hebrews12:5-6)

King David, the psalmist, had experienced bone-crushing discipline from God for his sin of adultery with Bathsheba and the killing of her husband by his order.

He speaks of it in Psalm 51:8,

"Let me hear joy and gladness; let the bones You have crushed rejoice."

Further down, in verse number 12, he pleads, "*Restore to me the joy of Your salvation.*"

David uses the Hebrew word 'yesha' (salvation, liberty, safety) to describe the joyous life of the sheep who remains near the shepherd, who stays on the path. He can run freely and eat whatever his shepherd prepares. He has no fear of harm. His shepherd will not allow him to stray too far, and he will use his rod to drive away enemies.

A heavenly Shepherd says this in John 10:14-16,

"I am the good shepherd. I know my sheep, and my sheep know me (just as the Father knows me, and I know the Father). And I lay down my life for the sheep. I also have other sheep that are not of this sheep pen. I must bring them also, and they will listen to my voice. Then there will be one flock and one Shepherd."

You may already be one of Jesus' flock or you may be one of the "other sheep that are not of this sheep pen." In either case, He is drawing you. It is intimacy that He desires. Come and see Him. Come and know Him. Come and follow Him.

COME AND PRAY

Dear Jesus, I think I may be one of those "other sheep."

I have heard about You. I have known some of Your followers who made me feel separate, not wanted. But Your words show something different. In talking about people like me, You say, "I *must* bring them."

I want to know You and to be known by You. I need Your protection, Your care.

Please bring me into Your flock and help me to be an obedient sheep who can live freely and joyously in Your presence.

Come and Know

"We have come to believe and to know
that you are the Holy One of God." John 6:69
"This is how we are sure that we have come to know
Him: by keeping His commands."
1 John 2:3

No one has ever seen God, but the one and only Son,
who is himself God and is in closest relationship with the
Father, has made him known.
John 1:18

"Come and experience this
God who so longs for you to know Him.
I keep asking that the God of our Lord Jesus Christ,
the glorious Father, may give you the
Spirit of wisdom and revelation so that you may know
Him better."
Ephesians 1:17

When I Am Afraid

Come and know that fear is a common experience. What is uncommon is how God wants us to handle fear, and grow from it.

"When I am afraid, I put my trust in you.⁴ In God, whose word I praise—in God I trust and am not afraid. What can mere mortals do to me?" (Psalm 56:3-4)

These words of King David indicate the reality of our fallen nature—which is to be afraid, and feel the potency of fear. Fear is like a warning light on the dashboard of a car. It appears because something around us is wrong and requires attention. When that light appears on my dashboard, I look at my vehicle manual to see what it means. Usually, there is some step that I need to take to correct the problem (put air in my tires, change the oil, etc.) Sometimes, when the problem is far beyond the scope of my abilities, I call a mechanic to set things right.

Although this analogy might seem to have nothing to do with fear, in my opinion, it perfectly elucidates on matters of the soul. When that warning light of fear rises up in my soul, I need to turn immediately to my God and put my trust in Him. He has the manual that reveals who I truly am and how I work best because He created me. He makes it clear that He has not given me a spirit of fear, but of power, love, and a sound mind. (2 Tim.1:7) And it is His insights that reveal to me how to turn to Him in fearful moments. Seeing the significance of this beautiful verse, I taught it to my sons to memorize.

When our second son was about nine, we planned a trip to Catalina Island. To reach the island, it was necessary to go by boat. Jonny was fearful of boats because as a baby he had been terrified by a boat's loud foghorn. That fear remained into his young life, much more deeply than I had realized it would. The night before our departure for Catalina, my sleep was interrupted by the bathroom light in our hotel room. When I went to check why it was on, I found our precious son kneeling over the toilet expelling his dinner.

Putting my arms around him, I gently asked what was troubling him.

"I'm afraid to go on the boat tomorrow," he replied nervously.

I noticed that Jon was gripping a small business card with wrinkled damp edges. Upon examination, I recognized this as the card our pastor had distributed at church that morning as part of his sermon. It was a passage from Philippians 4:6-7, which stated,

"Don't worry about anything; instead, pray about everything; tell God your needs, and don't forget to thank him for his answers.⁷ If you do this, you will experience God's peace, which is far more wonderful than the human mind can understand. His peace will keep your thoughts and your hearts quiet and at rest as you trust in Christ Jesus."

"Jonny, these verses tell you exactly how to trust in God when you are afraid. Let's do it together, son." I said to him, and after he nodded, I continued,

"You're worried about the boat, but God is telling you not to worry. Instead of worrying, God wants you to pray, telling Him your needs. What do you need God to do?"

"I need Him to take away my fear so I can sleep." He murmured.

"We know from Psalm 56 that when we trust in God, we will not be afraid. So, you can tell God you trust Him and thank Him for taking away your fear."

In those moments, I saw my little nine-year-old morph into a champion right in front of my eyes. By following God's instructions, he conquered his fear, slept peacefully, and enjoyed every minute of the boat ride to Catalina. Jon made many boat excursions to Catalina Island after that day because God freed him of his fear for good.

When we are afraid, not if—because there will be times in all of our lives when fear and anxiety creep in—is when we ought to look at that "dashboard light" to see if it is warning of a serious danger; of something that needs our attention. As we learn how to navigate our experience of fear, we must remember that not all fear is from a spirit. In certain circumstances, fear is a natural response to a dangerous situation.

Speaking from personal experience, I know that I have been afraid when I have done something wrong, and sensed punishment lingering in the future. Typically for me, fear surfaces when a new situation reminds me of something fearful that happened in the past. As a five-year-old I was bitten on the heel by a dog and had to have the infected heel lanced. From that point on, I became extremely fearful when faced with barking dogs. I remember once, when I was walking home from the school bus (in the days before parents met their children at the bus) and I encountered barking dogs. I felt myself go cold, as a wave of fear spread throughout me. Sometimes, I would see the barking dogs in the distance, and I would take a new route home.

When fear warns us in such a way it can be very helpful. However, the fear that becomes anxiety can be crippling and stunt our experiences. Psychiatrists define anxiety as a mental condition characterized by excessive apprehensiveness about real or perceived threats, typically leading to avoidance behaviors and often to physical symptoms such as increased heart rate and muscle tension.

As Bobby Conner said,

"You cannot medicate anxiety; you can only repent of it."

To cut off fear before it becomes anxiety, we can follow the psalmist's plan.

"When I am afraid, I will trust in You. In God whose word I praise – in God I trust and am not afraid." (56:1)

In other words, just as I took a route away from barking dogs, we can turn away from fear and toward God. An acrostic for faith that I saw highlights this decision.

Forwarding
All
Issues
To
Heaven:

Dear reader, I hope you find this acrostic as helpful as I did in overcoming your fear, and turning to God in the ways we have discussed in previous chapters.

If fear has invaded your soul for some reason, waste no time in running to Jesus. Put your whole trust in Him. If He is not yet your Savior, recognize that, according to your Creator:

- You are a sinner. (Exodus 20 and Romans 3:23)

- You need what Jesus did for you on the cross. (Colossians 2:13-14)

- Thank Him for His sacrifice. (Hebrews 13:15)

- Humbly submit to Him, confessing your sinful state. (1 John 1:9)

- Receive the infilling of the Holy Spirit who will be your Counselor and who will lead you into all the truth. (John 14 and 16)

COME AND PRAY

Dear God, I feel that my heart is softening toward what You are saying in Your word. I know that fear has gripped me, sometimes to the point of anxiety. I want to be free of that fear.

Your words encourage me to believe that it is possible. For now, I lay down any doubts, any misgivings that I have had, and place my trust in You. I see that harboring fear and anxiety has kept me from You. I believe it is true that the origin of fear is the belief that You are not good or that You are not there. Yet, your words show me the deception of such a belief. I choose to trust you this day, and for all days to come.

God Hears and Sees

Come and know that the God of the Bible is a God who shows His love by seeing our needs, hearing our cries, and responding with compassion.

"God heard the boy crying, and the angel of God called to Hagar from heaven and said to her, "What is the matter, Hagar? Do not be afraid; God has heard the boy crying as he lies there."
(Genesis 21:17)

What is curious about this passage is that the preceding verse indicates that Hagar is crying out, but it says nothing about her son doing so. It is amazing to me as a mother how God seems to hear the deep needs of the sons I am praying for when I pray. As a member of 'Moms in Prayer,' I join weekly with other moms to pray for our children. So many prayers offered are not what our children would have brought to the Lord, but God always knows what they need most.

I remember a specific occasion when my teenage son was seeking a position at a local video store where in his own words,

"He would work till 2:00 in the morning and could watch whatever movies he wanted."

Those were his desires, but God knew what was best for him. David's daily routine after school was a request, "Did the video store call?" Even though the consistent answer was 'no,' it nevertheless took a few weeks before he awakened to what was going on. With that, he pointed toward me and exclaimed,

"You've been praying!"

Like Hagar, I cried out, and God answered my son's true needs.

Hagar is a servant woman who has given birth to her master's son at the instigation of her master's wife (not even a Hebrew soap opera.) After nearly fourteen years, she has been evicted from Abraham's home and sent out into the wilderness, a scary place for a woman and child to be alone with only one day's provision of bread and water. It is certainly a time to cry out loud.

Amazingly, God hears the voice of the lad. One meaning of the Hebrew 'howl' (cry out) is bleating. Think of a cast sheep that cannot get up after falling down. This is how I envision this young boy who must now become a man to care for his single mom. As God hears this "bleating" sound of Ishmael's voice, He responds with a promise,

"I will make him a great nation."

After this powerful proclamation, God opened Hagar's eyes, and she saw a well of water.

Is something troubling you today? Have you been abandoned, rejected, betrayed, or abused? Hagar had experienced all this, yet she still cried out to Him. In the same vein, you should be specific about your pain. Cry out to God. He is a God who has ears to hear. And, just as important, He has a heart to respond to your specific needs.

Here is what the psalmist says in Psalm 142. Read his words and be assured that the God of the Bible is a God who cares about your needs. He created you with a destiny and a purpose. He longs to see that fulfilled in your life.

I cry aloud to the LORD;
   I lift up my voice to the LORD for mercy.
²I pour out before him my complaint;
   before him I tell my trouble.
³When my spirit grows faint within me,
   it is you who watch over my way.
In the path where I walk
   people have hidden a snare for me.
⁴Look and see, there is no one at my right hand;
   no one is concerned for me.
I have no refuge;
   no one cares for my life.

⁵I cry to you, Lᴏʀᴅ;
I say, "You are my refuge,
    my portion in the land of the living."
⁶Listen to my cry,
    for I am in desperate need;
rescue me from those who pursue me,
    for they are too strong for me.

COME AND PRAY

"Lord, I thank You that You are a God who hears. I need to have the assurance today that You see the scary situation I am in. Answer me when I pray, O God, my defender! When I was in trouble, you helped me. Be kind to me now and hear my prayer." (Psalm 4:1)

Your word assures me that I can trust in You. You tell me in Isaiah 65:24,

"I will answer them before they even call to me. While they are still talking about their needs, I will go ahead and answer their prayers!"

Thank You, Lord for understanding my need at this moment and for moving on my behalf to meet it.

The Lord, Our Banner

Come and know that God's covering is for those who revere him.

When Israel was away at war with Aram in the north, the country of Edom invaded them from the south. (2 Samuel 2:8)

Here is the cry of the Israelites to their God from Psalm 60:1-4:

You have rejected us, God, and burst upon us;

you have been angry—now restore us!

² You have shaken the land and torn it open;

mend its fractures, for it is quaking.

³ You have shown your people desperate times;

you have given us wine that makes us stagger.

⁴ But for those who fear you, you have raised a banner

to be unfurled against the bow.

Friend, have you ever felt that God has rejected you or mistreated you in some way? Have you meditated on your circumstances so thoroughly that it feels like God has abandoned you? Perhaps you were away doing God's work and found that the souls of your enemy had made inroads into your family. When our city experienced widespread fires some time ago, it was reported in the news that while a local family had gone to Mexico to love and serve those in need, their house burned down in that fire. They could likely relate to the psalmist's prayer.

Amazingly, their attitude was more like that of Job in his time of loss.

"The Lord gives, and the Lord takes away. Blessed be the name of the Lord." (Job 1:21)

Verse 4 of Psalm 60 speaks of the trust that resides even in these Israelites who cry out to God.

"But, for those who fear you, you have raised a banner to be unfurled against the bow."

Let's unpack that statement a bit. The Jews had accused God of being angry. He **is** angry alright, but with their enemies. God contends with those who contend with us. (Ps.35:1, Is.49:24-26)

When David speaks of a banner, he is speaking not only in battle terms of raising a banner or standard to indicate the securing of territory and claiming victory. In this same verse, David identifies one of the ways that God reveals Himself – as Jehovah Nissi, the Lord our Banner.

God is not a banner for everyone. In this particular battle scene, He is not protecting the Arameans, nor is He on the side of the Edomites. David makes it very clear that Jehovah Nissi unfurls His banner over those who fear Him, those who acknowledge His sovereignty and ruling power, and revere Him. He is a jealous God who requires that we love Him with our whole hearts, our whole soul, our whole mind, and all of our strength. (Mark 12:30-31) And why not? He has given His very life in demonstrating His love for us. He has every right to require our reverence as a sign of our love for Him.

All glory belongs to Him. All of our trust can be in Him. Our belief in His goodness can prevail in our thoughts because He is good and trustworthy. Here are some truths we know about this God to whom the Israelites are pleading in Psalm 60:

1. "He hears our prayers. "I waited patiently for the LORD; he turned to me and heard my cry." (Psalm 40:1)

2. *He is intentional about listening to those who call to Him. "Because He has inclined His ear to me, therefore will I call upon Him as long as I live." (Psalm 116:2)*

3. *"The LORD is good to all, and His tender mercies are over all His works." Psalm (145:9)*

4. "*Men shall speak of the might of Your awesome acts, and I will declare Your greatness. They shall utter the memory of Your great goodness, and shall sing of Your righteousness.*" (Psalm 145:5-7)

Furthermore, consider the following verses,

5. "*The Lord is good, a stronghold in the day of trouble; and He knows those who trust in Him.*" (Nahum 1:7)

6. *To the fatherless, He is a Father. To the widow, He is a champion friend. To the lonely, He gives a family. He sets prisoners free and leads them into prosperity until they each sing for joy. This is our Holy God in His Holy Place.* (Psalm 68:5-6a, TPT)

If you feel rejected, attacked, or under siege today, cry out to Jehovah Nissi, the Lord our Banner. Ask Him to defend you as He unfurls His banner against the enemy's bow. Take a moment to bring your troublesome thoughts to Him. Leave them with Him and reflect on who these verses say He is as a banner to those who fear Him. Let Him bring you to His banqueting hall, where He sets the table before you in the sight of your enemies and places His banner of love over you. (Song of Sol.2:4)

COME AND PRAY

God, there are times when I feel that You are angry with me, that You don't care that I am hurting, that I have dealt with trials and heartache, sickness and pain for a long time. Sometimes I even think that You can't provide what I need. But these verses tell me something different about You.

I want to believe them. Help my unbelief. I need You to hear my cries. I want You to incline Your ear to hear what I am saying. I have heard that You are a God who hears, answers, and works wonders. I need some wonders in my life right now. I am trusting You to unfurl Your banner of love over me and against the bow of the enemies in my life.

No Fear Under God's Wings

Come and know there is no need to fear the chaos surrounding you when you know the God who rules over all.

"He will cover you with his feathers, and under his wings you will find refuge; his faithfulness will be your shield and rampart. 5 You will not fear the terror of night, nor the arrow that flies by day, 6 nor the pestilence that stalks in the darkness, nor the plague that destroys at midday." (Psalm 91:4-6)

The metaphor here is that of a mother hen gathering her chicks under her wings for protection from all harm. This Psalm begins with the following words,

"Whoever dwells in the shelter of the Most High will rest in the shadow of the Almighty."

Dwelling in the shadow of the Almighty is a place of peace and rest. But, practically speaking, how do we dwell there? According to videos I have seen, the chicks run to the mother hen when danger is present. She is always ready to spread her wings wide and gather them to safety.

Like a mother hen, our God remains undisturbed by the calamities of our world, waiting patiently for us to realize that in Him is where we will find peace and rest from the trials and hardships that beset us. He calls out to us,

"Come to me, all you who are weary and burdened, and I will give you rest. 29 Take my yoke upon you and learn from me, for I am gentle and humble in heart, and you will find rest for your souls. 30 For my yoke is easy, and my burden is light."
(Matthew 11:28-30)

Sadly, this is not the picture of God that most people have. They don't see Him as approachable and caring. These are the words of Jesus, and when He says His yoke is easy, it means it is well-suited for us. And, the term light refers to his burden or task and how it can be driven as by wind. The Bible reveals the truth about God.

"The Lord is gracious and full of compassion, slow to anger and abounding in mercy and loving-kindness." (Psalm 145:8)

Are you weary, precious one, tired of the reports swirling around you? News headlines of restricted, monitored activity, bank failures, wars, rumors of wars, reports of unprecedented death rates? Are you overwhelmed by the pressures of our fast-paced way of living, burdened by the seemingly impossible decisions you must make? Are you ready to cast your burdens and anxieties onto God, who promises to sustain you? Always remember that He will never let the righteous (those in right standing with Him because they have put their trust in Jesus) fall. (Psalm 55:22)

Understand where God is amidst all that is troubling you in the world, and seek Him as the darkness swirls around you. Learn his perspective as shared in Psalm 2:2-6, which states,

"The kings of the earth rise up and the rulers band together against the Lord and against his anointed, saying, 3 "Let us break their chains and throw off their shackles."4 The One enthroned in heaven laughs; the Lord scoffs at them. 5 He rebukes them in his anger and terrifies them in his wrath, saying,6 "I have installed my king on Zion, my holy mountain."

As you navigate life in these noisy and chaotic times, remember that God is in charge. He rules and reigns. Earth's leaders can rise up; they can threaten this God. We see what happened to the ones who built the tower of Babel. Their lofty project failed. Their language was confused, and God scattered them throughout the earth. (Gen.11)

His plans are good; and they are for our welfare. Yet, he has given us the freedom to reject his plans at our peril. Jonah 2:8 elucidates,

"Those deceived by worthless things lose their chance for mercy."

We can become so distracted by the worthless things the world displays as enticing that we make choices that keep us from God's mercy that we so desperately need.

King David expresses this sentiment very well in 1 Chronicles 21:13,

"I am in deep distress. Let me fall into the hands of the Lord, for his mercy is very great; but do not let me fall into human hands."

Perhaps everyone you know is kind-hearted, has your best interests at heart, and is entirely selfless. This was certainly not the case for David, nor for me. David did not want to fall into the human hands of those seeking his downfall and would stop at nothing, not even his death. In Romans 3:10-12, the apostle Paul, quoting Psalm 14:1-3, alludes to what David was experiencing:

"There is no one righteous, not even one; there is no one who understands; there is no one who seeks God. All have turned away, they have together become worthless; there is no one who does good, not even one."

There are times when we feel this way about the humans we know. All of us have an inclination toward sin. God makes this clear in Romans 3:23,

"All have sinned and come short of the glory of God."

Once we accept this truth about ourselves and realize that there is a God who knows this about us and loves us still, we can turn to him with confidence that he will cover our sin confession with his gracious mercy. There are two words that you will often hear spoken by Christians. I want to clarify the difference. Mercy means that God does not give us what we deserve, which is eternal punishment for our sins. Grace means that God does give us what we do not deserve: forgiveness and salvation (deliverance, preservation, safety, as the present possession of all true Christians.)

Know that the God I am inviting you to know and embrace is One who has loved you with everlasting love. He has been drawing you to his Son Jesus longer than you know. The fact that you are still reading this book tells me that you have sensed the drawing and are intrigued. You want to learn more. You want to know Him. Perhaps you may find yourself in a similar situation to what the Psalmist learned:

"Whenever I am anxious and worried, you comfort me and make me glad." (Psalm 94:19 GNT)

"When I said, My foot is slipping, Your mercy and loving-kindness, O Lord, held me up." (Psalm 94:18)

Perhaps some other verses will help illuminate my point:

"There is no one like the God of Israel! He rides on the clouds in his divine greatness. He comes riding through the skies to help you." (Deuteronomy 33:26 ERV)

"Do not overlook the obvious here, friends. With God, one day is as good as a thousand years, a thousand years as a day. God is not late with his promise as some measure lateness. He is restraining himself on account of you, holding back the End because he does not want anyone lost. He is giving everyone space and time to change." (2 Peter 3:9 MSG)

This, my dear readers, is the heart of God who is waiting for you to be like the frightened chicks, to come and dwell in His shelter. *Why does he want this?* So that you will not fear.

COME AND PRAY

God, I am looking at some truths here today that I may not want to face. The world around me has renamed my sin, calling adultery an affair; the product of fornication, a love child; alcoholism, a disease; homosexuality, sexual preference; greed, ambition. But you are not fooled. You know how sin devastates my life, takes me farther than I wanted to go, makes me stay longer than I wanted to, and pay more than I wanted to—no wonder I am afraid. I have reason to be.

Thank you for making me recognize my sin, confess it to you, and turn from it by the amazing grace you give to all seeking refuge under your protective wings.

The Lord Rescues

Come and know that rescuing is a frequent activity of God in the Bible. Learn and understand how He does this for you, so that you may better gauge His light.

In Exodus 14:13-14 Moses told the people, "Don't be afraid. Just stand still and watch the LORD rescue you today. The Egyptians you see today will never be seen again. ¹⁴ The LORD himself will fight for you. Just stay calm." (NLB)

Easier said than done! God does not always take over, telling us to just stand still and watch as He destroys our enemies or holds them at bay. However, there are times, like this one where the odds are far from in our favor. After all, Moses was moving up to two million people out of Egypt with the full contingent of pharaoh's angry soldiers following rapidly behind. He had come to an impasse at the Red Sea. This was the time for God to intervene *immediately*. Moses exhorted his people with a powerful word of hope, but one that took great faith to believe.

It is in relation to Moses that I think back to November, 2003, when the Red Cross withdrew from serving in Baghdad during the Iraq War. I was part of a small missionary team that had entered Baghdad at that precise time in order to establish a house of prayer. My Israeli roommate had been interrogated for two hours due to a double passport issue. Gunshots, like a bursting popcorn machine, resounded outside our hotel night after night. As we entered the local colleges to share the gospel with young students, we were greeted by security guards wielding AK-47's.

Nothing aroused genuine fear in my heart until we drove into the center of a marketplace and found ourselves surrounded with

Iraqis peering into our car, blocking the way to move forward. Our leader began giving instructions for possible escape routes and a means to reunite after. We had come to Baghdad for God's purposes, making financial and personal sacrifices. And, we were prepared to be imprisoned or even to die there. But there was no need for that, for our God had dispersed the crowd as suddenly as they had gathered. There probably had been no evil intent to begin with, and we had just encountered the terrifying possibility of what could be.

When we think of Moses' words that his people would have to do nothing as God would fight for them, a typical response would be, "God only helps those who help themselves." While this is a commonly quoted statement, it is not found anywhere in the Bible. Much of what we need in this life can only be provided by a Sovereign God—air, water, sun, *life*. Man might be able to provide oxygen, water, and heat—but not for an entire planet! And that only relates to the physical realm. Love, joy, peace, patience, gentleness, kindness, goodness, faithfulness, and self-control are produced within us by God's Spirit, which makes them all the more important for us in the long run!

Let's just focus for a moment on peace, which is something desired by all who are facing fear and anxiety. In this story, God is rescuing his people out of slavery in Egypt where they have been building cities, tombs, and palaces for pharaohs for 400 years. Their enemy is too strong for them, much like we read in 2 Samuel 22:18-19,

"He delivered me from my strong enemy, from those who hated me, for they were too strong for me..."

God has a perfect plan for the deliverance of the Jews. In this case, God is saying, "All I want you to do is watch Me."

Sometimes we do not even recognize our own enslavement. In the times that we live in, we find ourselves numb, having learned how to cope with the sting of our existence. But God sees our enslavement for what it is and He has a masterful plan for our rescue. Much like the story in Exodus, Jesus destroyed our enemy and made a way for us to have fellowship with Him. That escape plan is found in Colossians 2:13-15,

¹³"You were dead because of your sins and because your sinful nature was not yet cut away. Then God made you alive with Christ, for he forgave all our sins. ¹⁴ He canceled the record of the charges against us and took it away by nailing it to the cross. ¹⁵In this way, he disarmed the spiritual rulers and authorities. He shamed them publicly by his victory over them on the cross."

In this way, God removed Satan's power to accuse us of sin and He openly displayed to the whole world Christ's triumph at the cross where our sins were taken away. No more slavery!

³⁵"Now a slave has no permanent place in the family, but a son belongs to it forever. ³⁶ So if the Son sets you free, you will be free indeed." (John 8:35-36) Jesus, the Son of God, has rescued all who believe in him from sin and death. Consider the following beautiful verses:

"Praise be to the God and Father of our Lord Jesus Christ. In Christ, God has given us every spiritual blessing in heaven. ⁴In Christ, he chose us before the world was made. He chose us in love to be his holy people—people who could stand before him without any fault. ⁵And before the world was made, God decided to make us his own children through Jesus Christ. This was what God wanted, and it pleased him to do it. ⁶And this brings praise to God because of his wonderful grace. God gave that grace to us freely. He gave us that grace in Christ, the one he loves." (Ephesians 1:3-6 ERV)

You have just read the amazing blessings that we have in Christ when we surrender our lives to him in confession and repentance. We come to God as children of our Heavenly Father. We have a permanent place in the family of God. In this verse, then, we find a wonderful metaphor for what happens when we make this decision to surrender. We lay aside our sinful ways and all that belongs to that way of life.

In exchange, God, as it were, fills our bank account with his riches in glory through Christ. When we place our trust in Christ for salvation, we receive a divine ATM card. The riches are in my account. I have the means of access, but I must use it by faith to obtain what God has for me. Hebrews 4:16 encourages us by stating, *"Let us then approach God's throne of grace with confidence, so that we may receive mercy and find grace to help us in our time of need."*

COME AND PRAY

Lord Jesus, You have done all the work of paying the debt for my sins. You took my sins on Your body and experienced God's wrath in my place, all before I even knew You.

I come to You humbly today, laying down my sinful ways and self-will. I agree that I am a sinner in need of Your grace. Thank You, Jesus, for fighting this battle in my place, one for which I was totally inadequate. You deserve the highest praise. I exchange the fear and anxiety I have felt over unconfessed sin. Now I receive the peace that only You can give. I declare with confidence that I am a slave no more! Because of Jesus, I have a permanent place in the family of God. Thank You!

Do Not Fear Sudden Terror

Come and know that all evil will be brought to justice. The eradication of evil will not be a pretty sight, but God shall be in control.

"Be not afraid of sudden terror and panic, nor of the stormy blast or the storm and ruin of the wicked when it comes [for you will be guiltless]" (Proverbs 3:25, AMPC)

In our day and time, the counsel given in the verse above seems to be uniquely suited to our predicament. Evildoers seem to be lurking in unsuspecting places, all around us, occupying a central position in our societies. With each passing day, we are inundated with stories of bombings, stabbings, vehicular murders, and homicides. This proverb addresses the downfall of the wicked, and the impact that such a downfall would have on those who witness it. The downfall of evil would be no straightforward and simple feat, because the means of such a downfall could evoke terror and panic, it will most likely be dramatic and publicized. In the contemplation of such a future, I am reminded of Proverbs 29:1 CSB, where the following is stated,

"One who becomes stiff-necked, after many reprimands will be shattered instantly—beyond recovery."

This was certainly the case with the pharaoh of Egypt. Even after ten plagues were exacted upon his people, he remained unmoved and defiant. His end came instantly, with no chance for recovery, or redemption, and led to a joyous scene of celebration, described in Exodus 15:1-4, as:

"Then Moses and the children of Israel sang this song to the Lord, and spoke, saying: "I will sing to the Lord, For He has triumphed gloriously! The

horse and its rider He has thrown into the sea! The Lord is my strength and song, And He has become my salvation; He is my God, and I will praise Him; My father's God, and I will exalt Him. The Lord is a man of war; The Lord is His name. Pharaoh's chariots and his army He has cast into the sea; His chosen captains also are drowned in the Red Sea."

When confronted with ongoing evildoers, we often find ourselves asking, "How long, O Lord, how long before you intervene?" Many passages in the Bible show us God's heart about this. He allows time for evildoers to repent. Speaking from my own personal experience, I am grateful that He gave me time to recognize the evil lurking in my heart and repent for it.

Jesus taught a parable in Matthew 13:24-30 concerning the fact that both good and evil coexist. Instead of trying to remove evil in its early stages, the farmer in the parable encourages his workers to allow both wheat and tares (weeds) to grow to maturity so that they could be distinguished from one another.

It seems that we are living in a day when evil has greatly matured to an insidious state. When confronted by evil, terror and panic are likely to arise in the soul. Simply reading those two words—terror and panic—can evoke a stirring in the soul. The question that we are left with then, is *what are we to do?* In the face of such terrifying evil, what action should we take?

The answer to such a question lies in God' justice. God is a just judge. He will deal with evil and evildoers. He has prepared eternal punishment for evildoers, who fail to repent and redeem their souls. Consider the following verses,

"Then he will say to those on his left, 'Depart from me, you cursed, into the eternal fire prepared for the devil and his angels."

"The Son of Man will send out his angels, and they will weed out of his kingdom everything that causes sin and all who do evil." (Matthew 13:41)

One ought to turn to Job 20 to remember the horrific picture of God's punishment for the evildoer who refuses to repent.

If we are present to witness the downfall of evildoers, how can we protect our hearts? God clearly instructs us, *"Do not be afraid."* In John 14:1, he counsels, *"You must not let yourselves be distressed—you must hold on to your faith in God and to your faith in me."*

This is a command. God would never command us to do something that we are unable to do. If it feels like you have no control over your reactions, turn to Holy Spirit to strengthen you. Holy Spirit is the one who produces self-control in you, and enables you to hold on to your faith in a time where evil encircles us.

Whether fear and anxiety originate from seeing the wicked brought to an untimely end or from natural disasters, it is important for us to learn how to deal with the effect of amplifying evil. We have a choice. Some are choosing self-medication. According to https://medalerthelp. org, depression statistics for 2022 state that,

- The disorder is most common in young adults aged 18–25.

- About 31% of people living in poverty have been diagnosed with the disorder.

- As many as 37% of university and college students in the US have depression.

- An astounding 66.5% of trans teens have depression, statistics confirm.

- Depression rates are three times higher among people with HIV.

- Every day, approximately 110 Americans take their own life, and about 3,500 attempt to do so.

From these statistics, it seems that many depressed and anxious people are turning to some form of self-medication, which doesn't even have a high rate of success. Yet, everyone, everywhere has access to the God who created them and who says this of his thoughts,

"For I know the thoughts and plans that I have for you, says the Lord, thoughts and plans for welfare and peace and not for evil, to give you hope in your final outcome." (Jer. 29:11)

Why shouldn't we turn to this God, the one who created us, who knows the feeling of our infirmities, who has loved us with an everlasting love? King David says this in Psalm 139:5 TPT,

"You have gone into my future to prepare the way, and in kindness you follow behind me to spare me from the harm of my past. With your hand of love upon my life, you impart a Father's blessing to me."

While statistics can be mind boggling, what really matters is how we deal with the avalanche of 'bad news' that circulates in our world? Am I running for cover, waiting until Jesus comes and makes everything right? Or, am I recognizing who is on my side? It is time for a clarification, and an amplified knowledge of our faith.

Jesus spoke about two paths in life: the narrow one and the wide road. *Which one are you on?* Here's how Jesus put it in Matt. 7:13-14,

"Enter through the narrow gate. For wide is the gate and broad is the road that leads to destruction, and many enter through it. But small is the gate and narrow the road that leads to life; only a few find it."

We live in a world that says that all roads lead to God, but Jesus clearly refutes that in this statement from Matthew 7. It is easier to believe that I can get to heaven or find God however I want, but this is not true. Jesus conveys a story about a wedding guest that apparently had that attitude. Consider the way in which he dealt with him:

"But when the king came in to see the guests, he noticed a man there who was not wearing wedding clothes. He asked, 'How did you get in here without wedding clothes, friend?' The man was speechless. "Then the king told the attendants, 'Tie him hand and foot, and throw him outside, into the darkness, where there will be weeping and gnashing of teeth." (Matthew 22:11-13)

Furthermore, consider this verse, too,

21 "Not everyone who says to me, 'Lord, Lord,' will enter the kingdom of heaven, but only the one who does the will of my Father who is in heaven. 22 Many will say to me on that day, 'Lord, Lord, did we not prophesy in your name and in your name drive out

*demons and, in your name, perform many miracles?' 23 Then I will
tell them plainly, 'I never knew you. Away from me, you evildoers!'"*
(Matt. 7:21)

We enter this world through the body of a woman. We enter
eternal life by means of the body of Jesus who was sacrificed on the
cross for our sins. Jesus said clearly, *"No one comes to the Father except
through me."* My prayer today is for you. Read it and, if you agree, pray
it for yourself. May you tread the narrow road to eternal life.

COME AND PRAY

Heavenly Father, I come to you today on behalf of the many who
find themselves reading the pages of this book. You put them on my
heart long before this book was in print. You did that because they have
been on your heart for all eternity. Open their eyes to see the dangers of
following the wide road of destruction. Lead them to the narrow path
that will take them to life.

I called myself a Christian for many years before discovering that
I was on that wide road. Thanks for opening my eyes to my sinfulness,
then granting me a spirit of repentance, forgiving my confessed sin,
and granting me eternal life. *Do it for them, Lord.* Grant them a chance
for redemption, too.

Judging For the Lord

Come and know God's prescription for overcoming all your fears.

*"Jehoshaphat lived in Jerusalem, and he went out again among the people from Beersheba to the hill country of Ephraim and turned them back to the LORD, the God of their ancestors. ⁵He appointed judges in the land, in each of the fortified cities of Judah. ⁶He told them, "Consider carefully what you do because you are not judging for mere mortals but for the LORD, who is with you whenever you give a verdict. ⁷**Now, let the fear of the LORD be on you**. Judge carefully, for with the LORD our God, there is no injustice or partiality or bribery."* (2 Chronicles 19:4-7)

How much fear would be eradicated in our cities if judges followed this prescription for their responsibilities? You must know of cases where judges were too lenient, and the criminal returned to society to perpetrate more horror on the community. Conversely, it has been discovered through the sophisticated DNA testing we have today that some people have been incarcerated unjustly.

Let us consider some positive aspects of fear of the Lord. It is both the beginning of wisdom and knowledge (Proverbs 9:10) and the hatred of evil (Proverbs 8:13). Everyone in the position of giving a judgment needs wisdom because lives are at stake. If someone is unjustly released, innocent people could be harmed. Similarly, if one is wrongly retained, their life could be destroyed. Further, every judge needs to hate evil as much as God does. But there lies the problem; judges are only human, with an evil, fallen nature. (*"The heart is deceitful above all things and beyond cure. Who can understand it?"* - Jeremiah 17:9). Without fear of the Lord, it is difficult to judge justly.

Fortunately, God has made His wisdom, which begins with the fear of Him, readily available to judges in a courtroom and anyone who calls on Him for it. You might say, "I thought this book was about overcoming fear and anxiety. Why would I want the fear of the Lord? I think I already have that. I got that when the nuns hit my hands with a ruler in school when I didn't pay attention. It came when I was dragged to church weekly while my parents stayed home and watched football."

Not at all, fear of the Lord is the very thing, when embraced, that eradicates fear from our hearts and lives. As David declared when he was running from Saul who wanted him dead,

"I sought the LORD, and he answered me; he delivered me from all my fears. ⁵Those who look to him are radiant; their faces are never covered with shame. ⁶This poor man called, and the LORD heard him; he saved him out of all his troubles." (Psalm 34:4-6)

"Fear the LORD, you his holy people, for those who fear him lack nothing. (V.9)

The pundits of this world greatly misunderstand the fear of the Lord. Yes, there is an element of dread to it. We are talking about the God of the whole world, the Creator of all, who says of Himself.

"Do not fear those who kill the body but cannot kill the soul. Rather, be afraid of the One who can destroy both soul and body in hell." (Matthew 10:28)

This is a God to be rightly feared. Jesus spoke these words to His followers as He sent them on a mission. They would face hardships, perhaps persecution. Jesus knew that if they had proper fear of God, they would have nothing else to fear.

Jesus went on to say,

"Are not two sparrows sold for a penny? Yet none of them will fall to the ground outside your Father's care.[b] ³⁰ And even the very hairs of your head are all numbered. ³¹ So don't be afraid; you are worth more than many sparrows."

There are two sides to the coin of fear of the Lord. On the one side is an all-powerful God who can destroy us with a mere thought. On the other is a caring God who cares unconditionally for those who revere Him and come close enough to know His heart. As the opening passage reads, *"with the Lord is no injustice or partiality or bribery."* Psalm 86:15 gives this description,

"But you, Lord, are a compassionate and gracious God, slow to anger, abounding in love and faithfulness."

Let's look at some of the consequences of those who fear the Lord. Psalm 25:12-14:

"Who, then, are those who fear the LORD?

1. He will instruct them in the ways they should choose.

2. *They will spend their days in prosperity, and their descendants will inherit the land.*[13]

3. *The LORD confides in those who fear him; he makes his covenant known to them."*[14]

Proverbs 2 teaches how to learn fear of the Lord and enumerates its benefits.

My child, listen to what I say, and treasure my commands.

[2]Tune your ears to wisdom, and concentrate on understanding.

[3]Cry out for insight, and ask for understanding.

[4]Search for them as you would for silver; seek them like hidden treasures.

[5]Then you will understand what it means to fear the LORD, and you will gain knowledge of God.

[6]For the LORD grants wisdom! From his mouth come knowledge and understanding.

[7]He grants a treasure of common sense to the honest. He is a shield to those who walk with integrity.

⁸He guards the paths of the just and protects those who are faithful to him.

⁹Then you will understand what is right, just, and fair; you will find the right way to go.

In the same vein, there are numerous passages about the fear of the Lord in the Bible. They are worth reading to understand this very misunderstood term properly. We began this chapter talking about the need for judges to make decisions based on their fear of the Lord. You may not be a judge, but you make judgments daily. Learn how fear of the Lord can help you find the right way to go and teach you to hate evil and overcome fear.

COME AND PRAY

God, I want to know You. I don't want to be afraid of You, but I want the fear of You that these passages speak of. I want to know Your heart, Your thoughts, Your ways. Please lead me in this. I honor You as my Creator. I thank You for loving me enough to send Your Son Jesus to die on the cross for me. Please help me to make the right judgments so that people are helped, not hurt, by my decisions.

Come and Follow

Passing along the beach of Lake Galilee,
he saw Simon and his brother Andrew net-fishing.
Fishing was their regular work.
Jesus said to them, "Come with me.
I will make a new kind of fisherman out of you.
I will show you how to catch men and women
instead of perch and bass."
They did not ask questions.
They dropped their nets and followed.
Mark 1:16-18, the Message

It is not enough to see who Jesus truly is, even to know
His heart. It is in the obedience of following
Him that we experience fellowship with Him.

Not Afraid of Man

Come and follow Jesus, for although man can bring harm to you, when you follow Jesus, he is **with** you; he is **for** you.

"The Lord (Adonai) is with me; I will not be afraid. What can mere mortals do to me" (Psalm 118:6)

These are the words Jesus and the apostles were singing as they went to the Mount of Olives after the Last Supper. The Mount of Olives is where Jesus was betrayed by Judas and taken captive by the chief priests, the officers of the temple guard, and the elders of the Jews. These were the very religious leaders who had been praying and waiting for God's Messiah, but failed to recognize him when he came in their very midst.

Picture the scene. Jesus had just concluded the Passover celebration with his 12 disciples. So much took place at that table which we call the Last Supper. We can find the details in Luke 22:14-30.

- Jesus had followed the ritual of a Jewish betrothal ceremony (engagement party). He was committing himself to his followers, present and future, as their Bridegroom. The church that he was forming was to be the Bride.

- He instituted communion, taking the bread and saying, "This is my body given for you; do this in remembrance of me." In the same way, after the supper, he took the cup saying, "This cup is the new covenant in my blood, which is poured out for you." (Finally, Jesus' followers understood how his strange words from John 6:41-69 could be accomplished.)

- Jesus washed the feet of his disciples, modeling for them what he was requiring of them. "Now that I, your Lord and Teacher, have washed your feet, you also should wash one another's feet." John 13:14

- Jesus identified his betrayer to John (13:18-20) and warned Peter of his impending denial. (Matt.26:31-35)

- He spent some time teaching, encouraging, and praying for His disciples who were still unsure of the events about to unfold. (John 14-17)

All of the apostles, except Judas, sang these words of Psalm 118:6 together with Jesus. They declared that Adonai, the LORD God was with them. They sang that they would not be afraid and chided, "What can mere mortals do to me?"

But, when push came to shove, even the accusations of a young Jewish girl and those of others standing near him, struck terror into Peter's loins, causing him to do exactly what his Master had foretold. He denied with an oath (or profuse cursing) that he didn't even know Jesus! Just then, the Lord turned and looked at Peter. That knowing look brought back to mind Jesus' warning that before the cock crowed Peter would deny him three times. At the realization of what he had done, Peter broke down with bitter weeping. (Luke 22:54-62)

Have you ever been there? I have been there more often than I like to remember. You believe in your mind that everything you are declaring and proclaiming with your mouth is what you truly believe, yet you doubt it in your heart. This is a spiritual principle that separates faith that produces works from mere words of faith. "Truly I tell you, if anyone says to this mountain, 'Go, throw yourself into the sea,' and does not doubt in their heart but believes that what they say will happen, it will be done for them." Jesus demonstrated this principle many times for his followers. Eventually, they were able to apply it. (Luke 10:19)

What I have learned about this is what Ps.118:6 says, The Lord (Adonai) is with me. He is master of all. Since the Master of All is with me, I need to turn to him for direction, guidance to accomplish his purpose for me in each situation. I have been called on in many circumstances to pray for healing for people. I believe that Jesus is both willing and able to heal. And, healing is a very personal matter. We see that in the Bible. Blind Bartimaeus was healed miraculously and immediately because he asked. The blind man of John 9 went through a different process, involving some action on his part. This tells me that there is no set formula for God's healing to take place.

God has used me to heal the pain of individuals suffering from HIV Aids, cancer, kidney problems, knee pain, and other illnesses. As many as I have seen healed, there are many more who have not been healed when I prayed. I myself have received healing from colitis, allergies, vertigo, and a blocked artery, to name a few. Yet, I have a chronic back issue that has remained for most of my adult life. I have concluded that this is something I do not have answers for, but what I do know for sure is that I can call on the One who is always with me and then do what he says.

When I was on the mission field in Ethiopia, I heard of one of our translators who had healed a young boy who had been deaf from birth and had never spoken. This story thrilled me, so I asked the healer, "Bushra, how did you receive the gift of healing?" "I was in a local village sharing that Jesus, God's Son, had come to save the people from their sins. Suddenly I was surrounded by strong men wielding machetes, threatening my very life! 'STOP!' I yelled. 'Bring me someone who needs healing. I will show you the power of my God.' They brought the most impossible person from the village. No one, including myself, had seen a deaf person healed. I called on God to make himself known to these people through the healing of this boy, and he did! For the first time in his life, sounds spilled from his lips. The crowd stood in awe and professed their desire to follow the God who healed this boy."

Bushra's very life was in danger by mortal men. He called on the God who was with him, believing in his heart that God would respond, and He was saved from imminent death and many from the village were saved from eternal death.

How can we bring doubt in the heart to agree with belief in the mind? Psalm 86:11 from the Message reveals that this was a struggle for David because of the prayer he makes to God. "Train me, GOD, to walk straight; then I will follow your true path. Put me together, one heart and mind; then, undivided, I will worship in joyful fear."

As you face fearful circumstances in your life today, search God's word for a promise he has given that deals with your situation and then pray David's prayer.

COME AND PRAY

Thank you, God, that you are with me. My life does not always reflect this truth. Train me to walk straight; then I will follow your true path. Put me together, one heart and mind with your heart. Then I will worship in joyful fear. Reveal your word that gives perspective and healing to my present situation so that my life can give joyful testimony to your faithfulness. Thank you, Lord. Unite my heart to fear your name.

Victory Over Spiritual Manipulation

Come and follow the truth that when we experience the manipulation of our destiny, we can find courage in God.

"And I looked, and arose and said to the nobles, to the leaders, and to the rest of the people, "Do not be afraid of them. Remember the Lord, great and awesome, and fight for your brethren, your sons, your daughters, your wives, and your houses." (Nehemiah 4:14)

Nehemiah, cup-bearer to King Artaxerxes, was commissioned by God to return from Babylon to Jerusalem to rebuild the walls of Jerusalem that had been destroyed during the Babylonian captivity. Because of God's favor upon Nehemiah, King Artaxerxes provided him with letters of explanation as well as time off from his assignment as cup-bearer so that Nehemiah could see to the nearly impossible task of rebuilding the city walls.

From the time of his arrival in Jerusalem, Nehemiah was faced with overwhelming obstacles and opposition. The local Gentiles offered formidable resistance to his attempt to rebuild Jerusalem's walls. At one time, the Jews themselves rose up against Nehemiah. Nevertheless, no matter what obstacles he faced, Nehemiah's response was,]

"The God of heaven will give us success." (2:20)

And He did!

Seeing one plan after another fail, the local opposition leaders hatched a new plot. One of these men, Shemaiah, reported to Nehemiah that his enemies were planning to kill him.

"Let us meet in the house of God, inside the temple, and let us close the temple doors, because men are come to kill you—by night they are coming to kill you." (6:10)

Here is Nehemiah's excellent response to their lie and spiritual manipulation,

"Should a man like me run away? Or should one like me go into the temple to save his life? I will not go!"

Then I perceived that God had not sent him at all, but that he pronounced this prophecy against me because Tobiah and Sanballat had hired him. [13] *For this reason he was hired, that I should be afraid and act that way and sin, so that they might have cause for an evil report, that they might reproach me."* (6:11-13)

Have you ever been the victim of spiritual manipulation? Usually, fear will be one of the tactics involved. Just as faith opens the way for an outpouring of grace, fear provides the environment for Satan's demons to lead the way to the sins of doubt and unbelief, independence and isolation.

I experienced some of this in a church where I served for a time. I had been asked to lead a city-wide Bible study. At the time, I was seriously questioning some of the doctrines of that particular denomination, so to avoid a conflict of interest, I declined the offer. Nevertheless, the leadership insisted that I should take on the role of teacher and after much convincing, I finally did. The study went along well with good attendance, people coming to faith in Christ, and marriages healed.

However, when it was discovered that I was looking into other denominations, I was called into headquarters, reprimanded, and told that I could no longer minister in any capacity in the church. Of course, I was still a believer and I was teaching from the Bible, but this denomination valued their doctrines above the word of God. Despite what happened to me at the higher levels of that denomination, I remained a close friend of my pastor till the day of his death.

Because all churches are led by human beings, there will be flaws in how things are done. Like Nehemiah, we need to keep our eyes on Jesus. Let us consider for a moment his reflection, *"Should a man like me run away?"*

What did he mean by a man *like me*? What kind of man was he? From what the Bible tells us, Nehemiah was:

- surrounded with God's favor as with a shield. (Psalm 5:12)

- operating under the authority of the ruler of the Medo-Persian Empire (Nehemiah 2:7-8)

- a man who knew that the source of his strength and moral courage was the Lord who is great and awesome. (Neh.4:14)

- and that His God would give him success. (Neh.2:20)

You may have experienced spiritual manipulation or even abuse in your past. You may be experiencing it right now. Take time out to consider what kind of person you are. Ask God to give you discernment regarding the situation you are in. If you are a disciple of Jesus Christ, then you must remember the following about yourself. You are:

- more than conquerors through him who loved us. (Rom.8:37)

- one in whom the Greater One dwells (1 John 4:4)

- the recipient of Jesus' promises: "Lo, I AM with you always, even to the end of the age. (Matt.28:20) and for He [God] Himself has said, I will not in any way fail you *nor* give you up *nor* leave you without support. [I will] not, [I will] not, [I will] not in any degree leave you helpless *nor* forsake *nor* let [you] down (relax My hold on you)! [Assuredly not!] Hebrews 13:5b, AMPC

If you have been the recipient of spiritual manipulation or abuse, it is extremely important that you don't allow the hurt to become an offense and, over time, a root of bitterness.

"See to it that no one falls short of the grace of God and that no bitter root grows up to cause trouble and defile many."

Hebrews 12:15 I say "over time" because this verse tells us that the bitter root grows up; it does not stay underground, hidden away in the locked vault of our hearts. NO, it grows up, causes trouble, and defiles many. This word *defile* is a Greek word that means to contaminate morally.

It is important to begin at the root, the **start**, that is, the place of the hurt. Bring your hurt to the One who heals the brokenhearted and binds up their wounds, as Psalm 147:3 tells us. He knows the feeling of your infirmities. He knows any part you had in the situation, as well as what was done to you.

"For God did not send his Son into the world to condemn the world, but to save the world through him." (John 3:17)

That word *save* is a Greek word that means heal, preserve self, make whole. It's God's heart to preserve you as He created you. He does not want your hurt to become an offense and eventually a root of bitterness, instead he wants there to be the light of faith illuminating your soul.

COME AND PRAY

God, I love Your heart.

As I am coming to know You, I see that Your thoughts toward me are thoughts of peace and not of evil, to give me a future and a hope. (Jeremiah 29:11)

You want to heal the hurt that I have cherished in my heart. Forgive me for holding on to this hurt and not bringing it to You right away. I forgive those who hurt, or even abused me. I place them in Your hands.

You are a just God. As I forgive others, so You forgive me. Thank You for Your forgiveness.

Who Is Your King?

Come and follow the King of all kings, and ask yourself— to whom do you give your allegiance?

> *¹⁹The people all said to Samuel, "Pray to the Lord your God for your servants so that we will not die, for we have added to all our other sins the evil of asking for a king."20 "Do not be afraid," Samuel replied. "You have done all this evil; yet do not turn away from the Lord, but serve the Lord with all your heart. 21 Do not turn away after useless idols. They can do you no good, nor can they rescue you, because they are useless. (1 Samuel 12:19-21)*

The story mentioned above occurred at the end of the period when judges ruled the Israelites. Samuel was the last of the great judges and he had appointed his wayward sons to follow him into that role. But the elders resisted their leadership. They said to him,

> *"You are old and your sons do not walk in your ways; now appoint a king to lead us, such as all the other nations have." (1 Samuel 8:5)*

In rejecting the human leaders that Samuel had appointed, the Jews were actually rejecting God Himself, who was their very Creator and their Redeemer. God spoke to Samuel about this, And the LORD told him,

> *"Listen to all that the people are saying to you; it is not you they have rejected, but they have rejected Me as their king." (1 Sam. 8:7)*

God next instructed Samuel to warn the people of all the cruel ways a human king would treat them. He said to him:

"This is what the king who will reign over you will claim as his rights: He will take your sons and make them serve with his chariots and horses, and they will run in front of his chariots. ¹²Some he will assign to be commanders of thousands and commanders of fifties, and others to plow his ground and reap his harvest, and still others to make weapons of war and equipment for his chariots. ¹³He will take your daughters to be perfumers and cooks and bakers. ¹⁴He will take the best of your fields and vineyards and olive groves and give them to his attendants. ¹⁵He will take a tenth of your grain and of your vintage and give it to his officials and attendants. ¹⁶Your male and female servants and the best of your cattle[c] and donkeys he will take for his own use. ¹⁷He will take a tenth of your flocks, and you yourselves will become his slaves. ¹⁸When that day comes, you will cry out for relief from the king you have chosen, but the Lord will not answer you in that day." (1 Sam. 8:11-18)

The people would not listen to Samuel since their minds were already made up.

"No!" they said. *"We want a king over us.* Then we will be like all the other nations, with a king to lead us and to go out before us and fight our battles." (V.19-20)

Somehow, the people had forgotten how their God, their King, had parted the Red Sea, saving them from the Pharaoh and his army. What about the battle of Jericho, where a fully fortified city fell to God's people in a day? The Old Testament is full of such victory stories, but these Jews wanted a king with skin on, a human king just like the other nations, and they chose to go their own way.

Have you ever been guilty of looking for help other than to the King of kings? Think about the time you received a frightening diagnosis from your doctor. Where did you turn? Did you turn to Google, Facebook, or another doctor? When I was diagnosed with a blocked artery, after the initial fear, my next inclination was to turn to Jesus and say, "Thank You, Lord, for letting me live a long life. My body is in Your hands. I am ready to meet You if You are finished with my life. If there is more for me to do, I need You to instruct me on my next steps."

Having turned to God for guidance, here are the insights that I received:

1. Have others pray for you.

2. When you have symptoms, say, "The life of God is flowing through my body and removing from my arteries all matter that does not pertain to life." These beautiful words are based on 2 Peter 1:3, which says, *"By his divine power the Lord has given us everything we need for life and godliness through the knowledge of the one who called us by his own honor and glory."*

3. Trust in God's word from Psalm 73:26, *"My flesh and my heart may fail, but God is the strength of my heart and my portion forever."*

After following these instructions for one month, I had to take a nuclear stress test. During this test, doctors took thirty pictures of my heart and found that there was no blockage in my heart anymore.

Am I saying that this is a formula for everyone to follow? No. However, I recommend that we turn to God first when we have a need. He has an answer. As our Creator, He knows best what we need, and He desires that we prosper. Your need may not be a health crisis. It could be a relationship disaster, job loss, or natural catastrophe that destroyed your home and livelihood. We face many trials and tribulations on this side of heaven, but we must find solace in God. Jesus has given us His word to instruct, comfort, and heal us,

"I have said these things to you, that in me you may have peace. In the world you will have tribulation. But take heart; I have overcome the world." (John 16:33)

In times of hardship, it is all to easy to turn to an idol (which is anything that occupies the place in our heart that belongs only to God). Different people have different idols. For some, it can be travel, food, and sex, while for others, it can be drugs, alcohol and excessive sleep. What matters is that we use this substance as a substitute for turning to God, the One of whom Psalm 107:20 says, *"He sent His word and healed them, and delivered them from their destructions."*

I don't want to manage my destruction and run away from the things tearing me down. I want to be delivered from them, once and for all! *How about you?*

You may have a difficult marriage or a job with a boss who makes your life difficult. Perhaps you have a teacher who is making unreasonable demands. All you can think about is your pain and how much you want OUT of this situation. But remember: the only true way OUT is through God.

COME AND PRAY

God, in my pain, I have turned away from You. I have looked to the things of this world to comfort me; all I have gotten is more pain. Please forgive me for turning from You. I am coming to You now. Jesus, your word in John 3:17 says, *"For God did not send His Son to condemn the world but to save the world through Him."* Thank You for not condemning me in this painful place. I need Your saving today. If you are ready, pray the following or in your own words.

1. I agree that I am a sinner. I confess my need of Your forgiveness,

2. I believe that You died to pay the price for my sins. I believe that You were buried and that You rose again on the third day.

3. Today I receive the forgiveness of my sins and Your free gift of salvation.

4. I receive the Holy Spirit who will lead me into all the truth and who will be my Counselor and my Comforter.

5. I declare that Jesus is my Lord and Savior and I commit to follow Him all the days of my life.

Arise and Go Up

Come and follow the truth that God always leads us to victory, given that we do not sabotage the win by our sinful choices.

"Then the LORD said to Joshua, "Do not be afraid; do not be discouraged. Take the whole army with you, and go up and attack Ai. For I have delivered into your hands the king of Ai, his people, his city, and his land." (Joshua 8:1)

But why should Joshua be afraid? He was a seasoned soldier, and now a commander of Israel's army, who had had a great win at Jericho. Furthermore, in this passage, God clearly says that He has delivered the king of Ai, his people, his city, and his land into Joshua's hand. To most of us, Joshua's situation would seem to be a cause for celebration, but he seems afraid of something.

To better understand what is going on with Joshua, we need to go back to chapters 6 and 7. Joshua had just returned from a stinging defeat at Ai. He had sent only 3000 men to take this relatively small city, but the men of Ai killed 36 of the Jews and chased the rest out of their city, resulting in humiliation among Joshua's troops. As 7:56 informs us, *"The hearts of the people became as water."*

What derailed this otherwise easy victory? Achan, of the tribe of Judah, had defied Joshua's orders to keep "hands off" the booty at the great victory at Jericho. Joshua's orders detailed how nothing was to be taken for personal gain. Instead, all was to be destroyed except for special articles that were to be taken into the Lord's treasury. The entire city of Jericho was being destroyed, including every living thing in it, except for Rahab and her family (a story for another day.) Imagine the chaos that occurred as the gigantic walls of Jericho were falling, screams filling the air as people and children were being slaughtered, as animals and livestock ran everywhere. In the face of such devastating chaos, Achan must have thought to himself, "Who will notice if I take a little silver, a bar of gold, and some garments?

What Achan did not know was there is no such thing as a little sin. Even if the sin somehow goes unnoticed by those around us, what about God? Will He not see? Of course, He will. Not only will He see, but He will judge the sin and lead us to repentance (which cultivates genuine sorrow for the sin, and a turning away from it) because He loves us too much to leave us in a state of perpetual defiance. Fortunately, we live on this side of Christ's birth. We live in God's new covenant where, unlike Achan, we are not stoned for our sin and burned along with our entire family. That may be what we deserve for what we have done, but in His mercy, God planned another way. We will learn more about that as we continue coming to know Jesus.

> *God said to Joshua, "Get up. Why are you groveling? Israel has sinned: They have broken the covenant I commanded them; they have taken forbidden plunder—stolen and then covered up the theft, hoarding it up with their own stuff. The People of Israel can no longer look their enemies in the eye—they themselves are plunder. I cannot continue with you if you do not rid yourselves of the cursed things." (Joshua 7:10-12)*

Two earth-shattering pronouncements are made here, in these beautiful verses. These pronouncements can be listed down as follows:

1. Sin removes our ability to defeat the enemies in our lives.

2. Our relationship with God is impacted by our disobedience.

Joshua followed God's direction on how to deal with Achan, but in doing so, he was filled with dread and apprehension. In dealing with Achan, he lost all courage and confidence, and found himself in a dark and uncertain place. *Can you relate?* Perhaps you have been experiencing years of hardship because of someone else's unbelief. Or maybe you've aligned yourself with an unbelieving business partner or even an unbelieving spouse. Alternatively, a Christian leader you trusted or one of your beloved children has fallen into a sin that has impacted your life adversely.

In life, there is no telling what difficulties or obstacles you may encounter. Oftentimes, these obstacles appear at moments when you were just about to experience a breakthrough. Now, instead of achieving your goal, you find yourself utterly defeated because of someone else's choice. In an instant, all the old, negative feelings return. "What is the use of it all?" You may wonder in these dark moments. "I give my all and this other person ruins it for me. I do not have what it takes to go back and try to do it all over again." And just like that, all my confidence dissipates into the thin air and my courage begins to falter.

As I ponder what it must have been like for this steadfast leader of Israel, Joshua, I honestly cannot think of anyone who has disappointed me in this way. Oh, yes, there were times when things my sons did or said aroused feelings of discouragement, but it was never anything to this degree. There was however, one young college student we brought into our home, who went on to choose her own deceitful path of life, all the while pretending to be truthful and honest. But, as I consider what it means to choose a sinful path that has the potential to hurt many others, regardless of how hidden it is, I think I must have been that person at times to my husband.

For years, I wore the label Christian with no resulting heart change, no true submission to Jesus Christ. The label without the surrender leaves plenty of room for sin, and may even lead to the cultivation of a sinful lifestyle. Because I was living for myself, I did not consider the effect my lifestyle had on others. I was selfish in my pursuits, and did not stop for a moment to consider how my blatant sin could slander my husband's reputation.

If you are sensing God's call to arise and go up, look to Him for support and strength. If He is calling you, He will equip and strengthen you. The psalmist in Psalm 62 can be your model.

"*Yes, my soul, find rest in God; my hope comes from him.*
⁶ Truly he is my rock and my salvation;
   he is my fortress, I will not be shaken.
⁷ My salvation and my honor depend on God;
   he is my mighty rock, my refuge.
⁸ Trust in him at all times, you people;
   pour out your hearts to him, for God is our refuge."

COME AND PRAY

God, I sense You calling me back to arise and go up to a dream, a challenge, a project I had tried before. You will not allow me to let past discouragement hold me back. I long to move forward, but fear keeps nagging at my memory.

Nevertheless, in spite of my fears and apprehensions, I will place my trust in Your words; I will pour out my heart to You. I will trust in You at all times. I forgive the ones who have caused me to fail in the past. I ask You to bless them and reveal Yourself to them so that their heart may change like mine has.

The Kinsman Redeemer

Come and follow the many facets of GOD THE REDEEMER. Learn of His great love for you, and understand it deeply.

"And now, my daughter, don't be afraid. I will do for you all you ask. All the people of my town know that you are a woman of noble character." (Ruth 3:11)

Have you been in a place where your safe and secure world suddenly broke apart? Surrounded by shattered pieces and fragments, have you found yourself at a loss as to how to rebuild with so much wreckage? If you have been in a similar place, then you will be able to relate to the plight of Ruth, the main character in this story.

Ruth, a woman of Moab, met and married a Jewish man named Mahlon who had moved to Moab with his family at a time of famine in his country of Israel. The family expanded as another Moabite girl, Orpah, married Mahlon's brother, Kilion. For Jewish sons to marry outside of their tribe, more so outside of their faith, was forbidden. Nevertheless, these were hard times. In time, all three men of the family, the two sons and their father, died. Naomi, the widow was left with the two Moabite daughters-in-law.

In my opinion, the truly amazing part of this story is how Ruth bypassed fear. With only women in her life at this point, she was in a dangerous position. Women had little standing in society, widows even less. All three were in an insecure position. As the overseer of the family, Naomi decided to return to her homeland, Israel. She encouraged her daughters to remain in their country and find new husbands. Ruth 1:8 gives a glimpse into the relationship among these women.

"Then Naomi said to her two daughters-in-law, "Go back, each of you, to your mother's home. May the LORD show you kindness, as you have shown kindness to your dead husbands and to me."

Even though Naomi urges Ruth to return to her own people and her gods, Ruth insists,

"Don't urge me to leave you or to turn back from you. Where you go, I will go, and where you stay, I will stay. Your people will be my people and your God my God." (Ruth 1:16-17)

I find traces of Ruth's story in my own life. As an orphan being raised by relatives, I felt insecure, as if I truly didn't belong, through no fault of theirs. It was just a feeling that was hard to shake. As I began reading my Bible and came across these words in Psalm 45:10-11, I suddenly had the light of a wonderful new perspective.

"Listen, daughter, and pay careful attention: Forget your people and your father's house. [11]Let the king be enthralled by your beauty; honor him, for he is your lord."

Through these words I felt that Jesus was talking directly to me, drawing me into an intimate relationship. I was even more assured by v.13,

"The king's daughter is all glorious within: her clothing is of wrought gold."

I felt that these verses were written for me because, after all, I was the King's daughter; Edward King was my father. The words "all glorious within" spoke to me of internal beauty, a beauty that is unlike the external, flashy display of the world.

I was loved by the King of kings. He saw a beauty in me that He desired. The One who has chosen me is *"the most excellent of men, whose lips have been anointed with grace, since God has blessed Him forever."* (v.2)

This wonderful King was calling me into His world; He was inviting me to belong to Him. At that time, I had no idea how this would be accomplished. Regardless, if Jesus was calling me to Himself, He would surely reveal more details when the time was right.

Ruth had set her heart on remaining with Naomi and attaching herself to the one true God. God rewarded her fidelity in the end with a prosperous husband, Boaz, who was a kinsman (near relative) of her former husband. Boaz redeemed (bought) the property left by Ruth's deceased father-in-law, thereby gaining the right to marry Ruth. His words in support of her convey Boaz' admiration of this newly discovered young relative. Consider the following verse:

"And now, my daughter, do not be afraid. I will do for you all you ask. All the people of my town know that you are a woman of noble character." (Ruth 3:11)

Boaz is called a kinsman redeemer because of his relationship (kin) and his ability to buy back (redeem) Elimelek's former property and take Ruth as his wife.

How does this relate to you? If your world is breaking apart through death, a dire diagnosis, a job loss, divorce, financial reversal, or the betrayal of a dear friend, know that you too have a Kinsman Redeemer. He is a person of great wealth, who owns all the silver and all the gold, and the cattle on a thousand hills. His sincere compassion causes Him to incline His ear to hear your cries. He loves you genuinely, and because of His great love, He has laid down His very life to grant you freedom from sin and death. His very wounds have released your healing. Remember that each time you encounter difficulty in your life.

This Kinsman Redeemer is inviting you into a relationship with Him if you have not already responded to Him.

"Come near to God and He will come near to you." (James 4:8)

"Humble yourself before the Lord and He will lift you up." (James 4:10)

These are the necessary steps to enter a saving relationship with your Kinsman Redeemer, Jesus.

1. Acknowledge that you are a sinner. Romans 3:23 *"For all have sinned and come short of the glory of God."* Look at the

ten commandments (Exodus 20) Can you say that you have faithfully obeyed them all?

2. Trust that Jesus has paid the debt for all of your sins.

"For God took the sinless Christ and poured into him our sins. Then, in exchange, he poured God's goodness into us!" (2 Corinthians 5:21 TLB)

"For the wages of sin is death, but the gift of God is eternal life in Christ Jesus."

3. Receive the Holy Spirit who is given to you as your teacher and counselor. As John 14:26 wonderfully reveals,

"But the Advocate, the Holy Spirit, whom the Father will send in my name, will teach you all things and will remind you of everything I have said to you."

COME AND PRAY

Dearest reader, I urge you to read this prayer. If your heart resonates with it, I urge you to pray it from the depths of your heart.

Dear God,

I know that I am a sinner and I ask you to please forgive my sins. I believe in my heart that Jesus is your Son; that He died for me on a cross, was buried, and you raised Him back to life. Jesus, I declare that you are my Lord and I open my heart to you. I receive the Holy Spirit who will lead me into all the truth and teach me how to follow You. I receive Jesus as my Kinsman Redeemer. Jesus, I choose to follow you all the days of my life.

Divine Payback

Come and follow the truth that vengeance is God's. Learn early on not to take vengeance in your hands; place your trust in God.

*"Say to those who have an anxious heart, "Be strong; **fear not**! Behold, your God will come with vengeance, with the recompense of God. He will come and save you."* (Isaiah 35:4 ESV)

To have an anxious heart implies that fear has dwelt there for a long time. How much fear is required to make a heart anxious? And what kind of fear would that be? Fear of the unknown, fear of the known, fear of people, fear of failure, fear of fear? What can we do with a heart full of fear? We can go, like David, to the Lord,

*"I sought the Lord, and he answered me; he delivered me from **all** my fears."* (Ps.34:4)

There is not one fear that escapes his deliverance. He fully desires our freedom from fear.

I remind you of 2 Timothy 1:7,

"God has not given us a spirit of fear, but of power, love, and a sound mind."

We see then that fear can be a spirit. Since God has not given us that spirit, it indeed comes from the enemy of our souls, which gives him access to our souls. Fear opens the door to him. When fear takes over, faith's foothold is dislodged. We need God's power to restore stable faith.

Isaiah 35:4 speaks of God coming with vengeance and divine recompense (payback.) It implies that the supplicant has been treated wrongly. Could that be you? Perhaps you've been overlooked for a much-deserved promotion or, worse yet, have been demoted. Maybe the love of your life has just chosen to break your marriage covenant for a liaison with another. Have you come to a place of desperation where all your efforts seem in vain?

No matter what challenges you may be facing, there is always a choice to be made. You may attempt to tackle the issue on your own, despite the fact that your efforts have been insufficient in the past. Alternatively, you may wallow in self-pity, creating fertile ground for bitterness to take root. However, there is another option - to place your faith in God's justice and patiently wait for His divine retribution to take hold. What might this entail? It may require you to humble yourself and patiently await God's timing, knowing that His plans are for the benefit of those who love Him and are called according to His purposes, as stated in Romans 8:28.

Many years ago, my husband experienced a major demotion at the university where he taught. At the time, he was head of two departments: Career Development and Continuing Education. His staff loved him, and he succeeded greatly in all his work. Suddenly, the board of directors ousted the founding president and brought in a new president who set about to remove all the "old guard," not unusual in such circumstances.

My husband, who has two master's degrees and a doctorate, was replaced with a person with only a master's degree. Then he was assigned to a virtual closet to write a staff handbook. A proud man would have seen the handwriting on the wall and rebelled. But George, being a humble man, set about the new assignment with diligence as was his custom. He didn't complain but accepted the work that was assigned. I was declaring Proverbs 22:29 over my husband's situation during this time.

"Do you see someone skilled in their work? They will serve before kings and not before officials of low rank."

Although George never served under kings, he did serve under the new president and was given the distinct honor of being the grand marshal at the university's graduation ceremonies.

After completing the handbook and presenting it to the new president, he received this accolade. "I am very impressed with how you handled this situation, George. As long as I am president, you will be on my team." Divine recompense! God's payback comes to those who humble themselves under his mighty hand that, in due time, he may exalt them. (1 Peter 5:6) George remained at the university for years after the president moved on. After 40 years of service, he retired with honor and dignity. His years of service were celebrated with a lavish retirement party hosted by the new Chancellor, Provost, and President.

I don't know what situation you are facing today that requires divine recompense. Perhaps you've been waiting long for payback for some perceived injustice. God knows the whole situation. He may be waiting for you to forgive the person who wounded you. I imagine that may not be what you want to hear. You might have recoiled at the thought of forgiving the "oppressor." I've been there. I understand, but I also understand that God requires our forgiveness for all the right reasons.

"Do not judge, and you will not be judged. Do not condemn, and you will not be condemned. Forgive, and you will be forgiven."
(Luke 6:37)

According to the Mayo Clinic, forgiveness can lead to:

- Healthier relationships that improve mental health
  Less anxiety, stress, and hostility.

While your emotions may recoil at the thought of forgiving someone who hurt you deeply, the act of forgiveness is obedience to God. It is not a means of accepting injustice. You are not saying what they did is alright and not a problem. Injustice is what God handles. Forgiveness is our part, for our sake.

COME AND PRAY

God, you know what happened to me was wrong and deeply hurtful. You see all sides of the issue. I am bringing it to you. Of course, my heart wants payback for the person(s), but I am choosing, by faith, to obey you and forgive them. I long for less anxiety, stress, and hostility in my life. I believe that it will come through obeying you in this matter. Help my faith to grow even stronger as I seek to follow You with my whole heart.

GOD'S PRESENCE, THE FEAR DEFEATER

Come and know that fear cannot exist in the presence of the Living God. His perfect love casts it out!

1Chronicles 28:20 David also said to Solomon his son, "Be strong and courageous, and do the work. Do not be afraid or discouraged, for the Lord God, my God, is with you. He will not fail you or forsake you until all the work for the service of the temple of the Lord is finished."

Here we have King David, the man who desired to build a temple for his God, but was denied the privilege because he was a man of war. David is here commissioning his son Solomon, a man of peace, who is God's choice for the building of the temple. David is encouraging his son to not be afraid or discouraged.

Why would Solomon be afraid of this task? He was a young man who had grown up in the king's palace and probably had little practical experience. After losing her first child with King David, Solomon's mother may have doted on him, sheltering him from hardship. He may have been hated by his brothers who considered that they were more rightful heirs to the throne. After all, Solomon's mother was Bathsheba, the former wife of a Hittite warrior in King David's army. She had entered into an illicit relationship with the king, at his mandate. His brothers probably considered him an outcast.

Are you in a situation right now where you are facing a daunting task? Perhaps you struggle with provision or resources. Or, maybe you are fighting internal, critical voices that highlight your past failures. Perhaps your experience is inadequate for the task you are facing. You may have people in your life who have nothing to offer but negative comments.

It is possible that you have never had a compassionate father who would speak such words of encouragement as David spoke to his son. Know that there is a Father in heaven who so loved the world that He gave His only begotten Son, that whoever believes in Him should not perish but have everlasting life. For followers of Jesus, we have a Father who has loved us with an everlasting love. Here is how Jeremiah expresses it in Jeremiah 31:3

"The Lord appeared to us in the past, saying, 'I have loved you with an everlasting love; I have drawn you with unfailing kindness.'"

Take a close look at those words. Even if you are not yet a follower of Jesus, God assures you that He is drawing you with unfailing kindness. The heart of this loving Father is expressed in the words of Zephaniah 3:17 AMPC

"The Lord your God is in the midst of you, a Mighty One, a Savior [Who saves]! He will rejoice over you with joy; He will rest [in silent satisfaction] and in His love He will be silent and make no mention [of past sins, or even recall them]; He will exult over you with singing."

Let's focus a bit on the fact that our God is in the midst of us. He is with us. His very name, Emmanuel, attests to the fact that He is God *with* us. Have you experienced times in your life when you faced frightening situations that you would never have entered without a parent or a friend who was with you?

As a fifth-grader who didn't know how to swim, I encountered a situation where my teacher said she would teach me. Her method was to push me into the deep end of the pool. I would never have agreed except that she was right there ready to retrieve me with a lifebuoy attached to a cord that she held firmly in her hands.

God will call us to projects, works, tasks that may seem impossible for us to do. In fact it is said that following Christ is not just difficult, it is impossible. It is impossible to do in the flesh, that is with our human nature. We can only be Christ followers by God's grace and the empowerment of the Holy Spirit, whom we receive when we surrender to Christ. Jesus makes this promise to us in John 14:16 *"And I will pray the Father and He will give you another Helper, that He may abide with you forever."*

Even the great men and women of the Bible experienced a need for God's presence to be with them in order to succeed in God's call on their lives.

Moses had this need when God called him to take the Jews out of Egypt. God promised in Exodus 33:14

"And He said, "My Presence will go with you, and I will give you rest."

Then he said to Him, "If Your Presence does not go with us, do not bring us up from here."

God makes this promise in Isaiah 43:2 that we can take for ourselves,

"When you pass through the waters, I will be with you; And through the rivers, they shall not overflow you. When you walk through the fire, you shall not be burned, Nor shall the flame scorch you."

God was faithful to this word when the Jews passed through the Red Sea and again through the Jordan River. He was faithful to the three men of Daniel 3:27 who were placed in a fiery furnace. God met them there and saw that not a hair of their heads was singed, nor their clothing scorched. They did not even smell of smoke.

Whatever work God has called you to, know that He is with you. As He said to Solomon, *"I will not fail you nor forsake you until all these works are completed."* I am trusting these words of the Lord for myself as I complete this book. God promised me at the outset that He is the Author. He is the Finisher. (Hebrews 12:2) I am made in His image and likeness. Therefore, I will finish this work because He is with me to complete it.

Jesus promises that He is with us always, to the very end of the age. Matthew 28:20b Take Him at His word.

COME AND PRAY

Lord God,

It encourages me greatly to know that You are with me, my refuge and strength, a very present help in trouble. (Psalm 46:1) No matter the size of the obstacle I face, You are GREATER. You are all powerful. You can do all things. No plan of Yours can be thwarted (Job 42:2) No matter if I feel weak and totally helpless, You assure me in 2 Corinthians 12:9

"My grace is sufficient for you, for My strength is made perfect in weakness."

The more I come to know You, Jesus, the more I want to follow You closely.

Come and Be Free

Then Jesus said to those Judeans who had believed him,
"If you continue to follow my teaching,
you are really my disciples [32]
and you will know the truth,
and the truth will set you free."
John 8:31-32, NET

"For freedom Christ has set us free.
Stand firm, then, and
do not be subject again to the yoke of slavery."
Galatians 5:1, NET

Jesus declared that He is the Truth.
Therefore, it is in surrendering to Him that we know true
freedom and a peace that the world is unable to give.

Whom Shall I Fear?

Come and be free and recognize that praise is the first step toward living a fearless life.

"The Lord is my light and my salvation—whom shall I fear?
The Lord is the stronghold of my life—of whom shall I be afraid"?
(Psalm 27:1-2 EHV)

If I have taken a stance toward praising my Lord, my eyes are on Him, not my circumstances. If I am considering the great I AM, then *who I am not* is of less consequence by contrast.

I cannot operate in fear and faith at the same time. Fear opens the door to Satan's tactics. We saw that with Job, who admitted,

"That which I greatly feared has come upon me." (Job 3:25)

In the same vein, 1 Peter 5:7-8 warns, *"Cast all your anxiety on him (God) because he cares for you. Be alert and of sober mind. Your enemy, the devil, prowls around like a roaring lion looking for someone to devour."*

Who is it, then, that the devil can devour? The answer to this question is simple and straightforward—the one who is overcome by anxiety because he did not turn it over to Christ. To allow fear to remain in our souls is a dangerous thing.

On the other hand, we read that it is impossible to please God without faith. (Heb.11:6) Therefore, the just (followers of God) shall live by faith. (Hab.2:4, Rom.1:17, Gal.3:11) The apostle Paul goes on to say,

"In him (Christ Jesus our Lord) and through faith in him we may approach God with freedom and confidence."

Where do we get this faith? Romans 12:3 tells us that God has given to each man a measure of faith. So, it is gifted to us. Another source, according to Rom.10:17, ESV, reports the following,

"So faith comes from hearing, and hearing through the word of Christ. Therefore, God has equipped His followers with faith. When we operate according to that faith we will be victorious....for everyone born of God overcomes the world. This is the victory that has overcome the world, even our faith."

King David, known for victory in battle, states in Psalm 34:1, *"I will extol the Lord at all times; His praise will always be on my lips."*

Considering his stance against the giant Goliath, I would have considered David fearless. Yet, he goes on in v.4 to admit, *"I sought the Lord, and He answered me; He delivered me from all my fears."*

Considering Kind David's words, we realize that fear is a natural emotion. It's what we do with it that matters. We can choose faith by praising God no matter what, or we can give in to fear and let the devil devour us.

There are times in life when fear overtakes us, especially when danger looms and we sense that we have no control. It could be a sudden reversal (job loss, divorce, a death or disability, a sick loved one, or a natural disaster.) In such times, our resources may seem utterly inadequate.

But there is One whose resources never fail. He is El Shaddai, the All-Sufficient God. When God identifies Himself as I AM WHO I AM, He includes the many aspects of His being: light, saving, power, eternity, peace, fatherhood, redemption, truth, sufficiency, and life! Remember: whatever you need in life is what God already IS. When I call upon Him and trust in Him, whom should I fear?

As young David assessed his woefully inadequate weapons compared to Goliath's full armor, he chose instead to draw upon the great I AM. David called out to the mighty giant,

"You come against me with sword and spear and javelin, but I come against you in the name of the LORD Almighty, the God of the armies of

Israel, whom you have defied. ⁴⁶The Lord will deliver you into my hands this day, and I will strike you down and cut off your head. This very day I will give the carcasses of the Philistine army to the birds and the wild animals, and the whole world will know that there is a God in Israel. ⁴⁷All those gathered here will know that it is not by sword or spear that the Lord saves; for the battle is the Lord's, and he will give all of you into our hands." (1 Samuel 17:45-47)

David chose to operate in faith, and God gave him victory.

Psalm 8:2 affirms why praise is a first step toward living a fearless life. "Through the praise of children and infants, you have established a stronghold against your enemies, to silence the foe and the avenger."

Against the face of our spiritual enemies, praise is like a stun gun. If the praise of children can establish a stronghold against the enemy, of whom then, should we be afraid?

When the enemy had leveled an attack against Paul and Silas for their preaching in Philippi, the two evangelists, beaten and bloodied, began singing praises to God at midnight from the prison where they were held in stocks. Here is the response God made to their faith choice,

"Suddenly, there was such a violent earthquake that the foundations of the prison were shaken. At once all the prison doors flew open, and everyone's chains came loose." Acts 16:26 The jailer called for lights, rushed in, and fell trembling before Paul and Silas. ³⁰He then brought them out and asked, "Sirs, what must I do to be saved?"³¹They replied, "Believe in the Lord Jesus, and you will be saved—you and your household."

My dear and precious readers, take your time to learn who God truly is. His names reveal His character. His word describes His thoughts and His ways. Choose to praise Him throughout the day. It is not difficult. When you see a beautiful sunset, say, "God, You created that. You are an amazing artist." In a trying situation, reiterate to yourself,

"God, you are my strength; I need You now."

When your day is blessed and going well, "Thank You, God, for Your presence and care."

COME AND PRAY

God, I love the simplicity of these truths. When faced with a dilemma, I have a choice. Will I choose to let fear overwhelm me and open the door to Satan? Or, will I choose to look up and praise You, thus activating my faith? Lord God, El Shaddai, I commit to make the latter choice. This is the way to victory over fear.

Requirements For Protection

Come and be free, knowing the importance of obe**die**nce. As we die to ourselves, we live under God's protection.

*"So **do not fear** for I AM with you; do not be dismayed for I AM your God. I will strengthen you and help you; I will uphold you with my righteous right hand."* (Isaiah 41:10)

The people of Israel had consistently disobeyed God's clear commands. At this point in their history, they were about to be disciplined. Nebuchadnezzar, king of Babylon, would take them into captivity after destroying their temple and much of the land of Israel. Although God had orchestrated this discipline, he wanted to comfort his people with the knowledge that he would be with them through it all. The footnote for this verse in my Bible reads, "The seeds of comfort may take root in the soil of adversity."

Because Israel had not been faithful to observe God's clear command to let their land lie fallow every seventh year, the people were assigned to seventy years of captivity, one year for every year that they failed to let the land rest. He is precise when God gives a command, and there are consequences for not following those commands.

"For six years sow your fields, and for six years prune your vineyards and gather their crops. ⁴ But in the seventh year the land is to have a year of sabbath rest, a sabbath to the L ORD*. Do not sow your fields or prune your vineyards. ⁵ Do not reap what grows of itself or harvest the grapes of your untended vines. The land is to have a year of rest."* (Leviticus 25:3-5)

And,

"Follow my decrees and be careful to obey my laws, and you will live safely in the land." v.18

The people did not follow God's decrees and obey his laws carefully, so they could no longer live safely in the land. Thankfully God is not only just—requiring justice—but also merciful and compassionate, as every good father would be. Isaiah 41:10 is a perfect example of these characteristics. Although God would not veer from punishing his people's disobedience, he offered them hope and comfort *before* the devastation occurred.

Are you facing consequences today for your choice in opposition to God's commands? Oh, I wish I could answer "NO" to that question. Unfortunately, I brought elements of death and devastation into my life and family through sins of the flesh before I became a born-again follower of Jesus. I said No to God's ways numerous times, and there have been consequences.

Even after becoming Jesus' follower, I failed to follow completely. As the mom of a strong-willed child, I sought God for his ideas on how to train him and how he should go. God gave me specific things to do, which I wrote down and then failed to do. Somehow, in my ignorance or perhaps my strong will, I thought my ways were easier. My disobedience paved the way for many difficult years with my son.

So, where is the hope in all this? What about all the talk of commands, consequences, and punishment? The hope for me was found in Lamentations 3:22-23,

"Because of the LORD's great love, we are not consumed, for his compassions never fail.²³ They are new every morning; great is your faithfulness. Each morning, just like dew on the grass, or the sweet song of birds, or the rays of the sun beaming through the clouds, God comes to meet us with fresh compassion, new mercy—all for the taking. If not for his love, I would be consumed."

Even as the people of Israel were looking ahead to the prospect of devastating exile, God gave them the comforting words of Isaiah 41:10,

"So do not fear, for I AM with you."

Here, God presents himself as Emmanuel, God with us, centuries before he would come in human flesh to be "with us." That preposition with, although seemingly insignificant, carries with it the connotations of:

- Agreement or sympathy

- On the side of

- Accompaniment, presence, or addition

- The means, cause, agent, and instrumentality of I AM with you, the God of the present moment. *"He is a very present help in trouble."* (Psalm 46:1)

He empathizes with your situation. He is on your side, accompanying you through the difficult journey of facing the consequences of your disobedience. He is the means of your proper outcome. By his grace and favor, secured by the death and resurrection of Jesus, we can receive God's strength and help. We can proceed securely with God holding us with his righteous right hand.

Even more than that, God gives us hope for restoration. He says in Joel 2:25 AMPC,

"And I will restore or replace for you the years that the locust has eaten—the hopping locust, the stripping locust, and the crawling locust, My great army which I sent among you."

How can God bring restoration to those who intentionally disobeyed him? Once we recognize our sin, confess it, and turn from it, his forgiveness is lavished on us. We are not crushed beneath the weight of our sin because of Jesus' obedience as expressed in Isaiah 53:10, GNT.

The Lord says, *"It was my will that he should suffer; his death was a sacrifice to bring forgiveness. And so, he will see his descendants; he will live a long life, and through him my purpose will succeed."*

COME AND PRAY

God Almighty, Lord of heaven and earth, your love is beyond anything I have witnessed in this world. All of your commands are meant to protect me and those around me. Your discipline is like that of a shepherd who pulls his straying sheep back to the path of safety. You know what will cause us to fulfill our destiny and bring glory to you. Forgive me for taking so long to embrace your commands and view them as safeguards rather than restraints. Because of my faith in Jesus, I am assured that You are the God who is with me, who strengthens and helps me, and upholds me with your righteous right hand.

God Makes Our Enemies Fear

Come and be free and see that God doesn't want us to be afraid. He makes our enemies tremble and protects us.

> *God! Arise with awesome power, and every one of*
> *Your enemies will scatter in fear!* (Psalm 68:1)

All through the Bible, we can see the truth of God's magnificence revealed. As the world grows dark and insidious, we may find it hard to see the light, but all we need to do is place our faith in God. But first, we need to know who God's enemies are. In this Psalm, they are referred to as God-haters and the wicked. Elsewhere they are called evildoers (2 Samuel 3:39), lovers of darkness (John 3:19), and lovers of the world (James 4:4).

The first evidence of God's defeat of His enemies is through the flood in Genesis 6-9. Through Noah, God spent a hundred and twenty years preparing for the destruction of the people of his day who are described in this way, *"Then the Lord saw that the wickedness of man was great in the earth and that every intent of the thoughts of his heart was only evil continually."* (Gen.6:5)

In spite of Noah's example of doing everything the Lord had commanded him in preparation for impending destruction, the people were eating and drinking, marrying and giving in marriage until the day Noah entered the ark. Since there had never been rain on the earth before this time, and because Noah was building an enormous sea-faring vessel many miles from the nearest body of water, the people must have thought he was crazy. It wasn't until Noah and his family were safely in the ark that God shut the door, finalizing the doom of the people who were apparently unmoved by Noah's example.

The Bible has numerous other examples of God arising in might and power against His enemies. Below are just a few examples:

Babel – Genesis 11:1-4:

"Now the whole world had one language and a common speech. ²As people moved eastward, they found a plain in Shinar and settled there. ³They said to each other, "Come, let's make bricks and bake them thoroughly." They used brick instead of stone, and tar for mortar. ⁴Then they said, "Come, let us build ourselves a city, with a tower that reaches to the heavens, so that we may make a name for ourselves; otherwise, we will be scattered over the face of the whole earth." We can see that God was not pleased with their plans by what transpired next. *So the Lord scattered them from there overall the earth, and they stopped building the city. ⁹That is why it was called Babel—because there the Lord confused the language of the whole world. From there the Lord scattered them over the face of the whole Earth."* (v.8-9)

Jehoshaphat – 2 Chronicles 20:

"The men from Ammon, Moab, and Mt. Seir rose up against God's people who were living in peace. Through King Jehoshaphat, the people fasted and sought God's help. They worshipped and praised their God, putting all their trust in Him. "As they began to sing and praise, the Lord set ambushes against the men of Ammon and Moab and Mount Seir who were invading Judah, and they were defeated. ²³The Ammonites and Moabites rose up against the men from Mount Seir to destroy and annihilate them. After they finished slaughtering the men from Seir, they helped to destroy one another." (v.22-23)

David – As we saw in 1 Samuel 17, David came against Goliath in the name of the Lord and killed the giant with his own sword.

Angel of the Lord – In the passage cited below, the Assyrians are bullying King Hezekiah of Judah. Again, we see God rising up in power and might to defeat His enemies.

"I will defend this city and save it, for my sake and for the sake of David my servant.35 That night the angel of the Lord went out and put to death a hundred and eighty-five thousand in the Assyrian camp.

When the people got up the next morning—there were all the dead bodies!" (2 Kings 19:34-35)

Jericho – When the people of God arrived at the Promised Land, their first challenge was the walled city of Jericho. Two spies went in to check out the territory. This is what they were told by the prostitute Rahab,

"We have heard how the Lord dried up the water of the Red Sea for you when you came out of Egypt, and what you did to Sihon and Og, the two kings of the Amorites east of the Jordan, whom you completely destroyed. 11 When we heard of it, our hearts melted in fear and everyone's courage failed because of you, for the Lord your God is God in heaven above and on the earth below."
(Joshua 2:10-11)

Dear reader, rejoice, for this is the mighty God of the Bible. Fear belongs to His enemies, not to His children. This is what God says in Deuteronomy 33:27 of those who belong to Him,

"The eternal God is your refuge, and underneath are the everlasting arms. He will drive out your enemies before you, saying, 'Destroy them!'"

The high priest Zechariah spoke these praises to God in Luke 1:68-74,

"Praise be to the Lord, the God of Israel, because he has come to his people and redeemed them. He has raised up a horn of salvation for us in the house of his servant David (as he said through his holy prophets of long ago), salvation from our enemies and from the hand of all who hate us—to show mercy to our ancestors and to remember his holy covenant, the oath he swore to our father Abraham: to rescue us from the hand of our enemies, and to enable us to serve him without fear."

God drives out the enemies of His people so that they can serve Him without fear. Remember, "God has not given us a spirit of fear, but of power, love, and a sound mind." 2 Timothy 1:7 When we surrender to His love, acknowledging our sin, turning from it, and receiving His forgiveness through Jesus, we become members of God's family. (John

1:12) These stories provide an example of God's mighty power and how it strikes fear in the camp of His enemies.

Many of us tend to view our enemies as those who belittle us at work in order to advance their own careers, or perhaps as our neighbors who spread rumors about us behind our backs. We may even consider those with different political or religious beliefs as adversaries. However, the Bible offers a distinct perspective on the matter. In Ephesians 6:12 CEB, it is written that "our struggle is not against flesh and blood, but against the rulers, against the authorities, against the powers of this dark world and against the spiritual forces of evil in the heavenly realms." Thus, regardless of who we perceive as our enemies, if we place our faith in God, He will provide us with the tools necessary to emerge victorious.

Regardless of who are enemies are, when we turn to God and put our trust in Him, He will equip us to defeat them. All we need to do is place our faith in Him.

COME AND PRAY

God, arise with awesome power, and your enemies will scatter in fear. I trust in Your ability, but also in Your desire to be my refuge at this time. Teach me who my true enemies are and how to use my authority in Christ to defeat them. Holy Spirit, warn me if I ever stray in such a way as to become an enemy of my God. Grant me a spirit of repentance in order to remain God's friend.

Slaves No More

Come and be free in the recognition that your freedom was not free; Christ paid for it with his life.

The Spirit you received does not make you slaves, so that you live in
__fear__ again; rather, the Spirit you received brought about your
adoption to sonship. And by him we cry, "Abba, Father." (Romans 8:15)

³They answered him, "We are Abraham's descendants and have
never been slaves of anyone. How can you say that we shall be set free?"

³⁴Jesus replied, "Very truly I tell you, everyone who sins is a slave
to sin. ³⁵Now a slave has no permanent place in the family, but a son
belongs to it forever. ³⁶So if the Son sets you free, you will be free
indeed. (John 8:3, 34-36)

I am concluding this scripture journey with verses on slavery versus freedom in Christ because if we want to be truly free, it is important to know what has enslaved us. Much like the Jews in this passage, when confronted with slavery, we recoil and back away in denial. *"I have never been a slave of anyone."*

When I was enslaved to sin and debauchery, that is precisely how I felt. As Proverbs 30:20 ERV says of the adulteress,

"A woman who is not faithful to her husband acts innocent. She eats,
wipes her mouth, and says she has done nothing wrong."

In my sinful life before Christ, I harbored the delusion that I was "calling the shots" in my life, and thought I was free. The only hindrance I felt was emptiness. I felt as though there was a huge hole in my soul that nothing in this world could fill. With every passing day, that hole grew and expanded, becoming so vast, that I began to hope for death. I wished that I would not wake up the next morning, or that someone would cross over the freeway and hit me head-on.

As my desire for ending my life illustrates, my journey from slavery to freedom was long and arduous. Seeing that misery loves company, I associated with other "empty souls" who also didn't know Jesus. To fill up the void brimming inside of our hearts, we involved ourselves in seances, tarot card readings, and metaphysical retreats. I was blinded by my ignorance, so that I didn't see any adverse effect that this might have on my marriage or my young child. Eventually, I found myself with a lack of maternal feelings for my baby, whom I was carrying in the womb during a metaphysical retreat. All my thoughts were pervaded by suicidal inclinations.

I sought relief through the church of my childhood. While religion was not the answer, a genuine relationship with Jesus Christ was what I experienced through a loving group of born-again believers in that church. They helped me to realize that I was "on the outside looking in" to the joy of knowing Jesus in a way that would make me a permanent member of the family of God and no longer a slave to my sinful and negligent nature. Though I had not seen myself as a sinner in the past, and certainly not a slave, God's word made it clear that I was.

"All have sinned and come short of the glory of God."

Those words from Romans 3:23 cut through the deception in my mind and heart, and prepared me to confess my many sins, and turn from them by God's strength.

Pastor John Piper, in his book <u>The Passion of Jesus Christ,</u> states, *"Sin is such a powerful influence in our lives that we must be liberated by God's power, not by our willpower."* Galatians 5:1 encourages us with this truth,

"It is for freedom that Christ has set us free. Stand firm, then, and do not let yourselves be burdened again by a yoke of slavery."

Jesus Christ took the burden of our sins on the cross so that we could be free of guilt and condemnation. Jesus paid a debt he didn't owe because we owed a debt that we couldn't pay. Our thanks and gratefulness to him comes in the form of obedience to his ways, his commands as revealed in his word, the Bible.

> *"As long as you did what you felt like doing, ignoring God, you didn't have to bother with right thinking or right living, or right anything for that matter. But do you call that a free life? What did you get out of it? Nothing you are proud of now. Where did it get you? A dead end. But now that you have found you don't have to listen to sin tell you what to do, and have discovered the delight of listening to God telling you, what a surprise! A whole, healed, put-together life right now, with more and more of life on the way! Work hard for sin your whole life and your pension is death. But God's gift is real life, eternal life, delivered by Jesus, our Master."*
> (Romans 6:21-23, the Message)

Speaking from personal experience, when I admitted my sinful state and sought God's forgiveness through Jesus, I felt a wonderful transformation take place. It was as though in a moment, my life went from dull black and white to vivid technicolor. Before, shrouded in sinfulness, my default mode was toward self-will and self-indulgence.

When I surrendered to Jesus, I had a new default – toward right living as I found it described in the Bible. I can remember viewing movies I had enjoyed before my life with Jesus, only to be repulsed by them after the Holy Spirit was living in me. My interests, my desires, my perspective had changed. I had been born anew.

We must hold dear to our hearts, value and care for the freedom we receive in Christ. Our freedom is not a license to do whatever we please. As the apostle Paul counseled new believers:

> [15]*"What then? Shall we sin because we are not under the law but under grace? By no means!* [16]*Don't you know that when you offer yourselves to someone as obedient slaves, you are slaves of the one you obey—whether you are slaves to sin, which leads to death, or to obedience, which leads to righteousness?* [17]*But thanks be to God that, though you used to be slaves to sin, you have come to obey from your heart the pattern of teaching that has now claimed your allegiance.* [18]*You have been set free from sin and have become slaves to righteousness.*

¹⁹I am using an example from everyday life because of your human limitations. Just as you used to offer yourselves as slaves to impurity and to ever-increasing wickedness, so now offer yourselves as slaves to righteousness leading to holiness. ²⁰When you were slaves to sin, you were free from the control of righteousness. *²¹What benefit did you reap at that time from the things you are now ashamed of? Those things result in death! ²²But now that you have been set free from sin and have become slaves of God, the benefit you reap leads to holiness, and the result is eternal life."* (Romans 6:15-22)

It was Jesus Christ who provided this freedom, as described in Galatians 4:7,

*"So you are no longer a **slave**, but God's child; and since you are his child, God has made you also an heir." Paul goes on to explain the need for Jesus to become a human. "These children are people with physical bodies. So, Jesus himself became like them and had the same experiences they have. Jesus did this so that, by dying, he could destroy the one who has the power of death—the devil. 15 Jesus became like these people and died so that he could free them. They were like slaves all their lives because of their fear of death."* (Hebrews 2:14-15 ERV)

At the close of the chapter, I would like you, my dearest reader, to take note of this truth, and embrace it wholeheartedly—Jesus died so that he could free us. *What could be more loving than that?*

COME AND PRAY

Almighty God, I see that for years I have had such a wrong picture of who you are. I was trapped by a spirit of religion. Even though I couldn't identify it, I knew in my heart that I didn't want anything to do with it. The spirit of religion taught me to follow man's way to reach you. You taught me that no one can come to You except through Jesus.

Forgive me, dear God, for taking so long to discover the truth about you and about the price that Jesus paid so that I could be free. I have put my faith in Jesus for my salvation, I commit to live my life in such a way that it fulfills your plans for me and brings glory and honor to you.

I thank you for the Holy Spirit who will lead me into all the truth and remind me of all that Jesus has taught me, and who will pray for me when I don't know what to pray for. He empowers me to live in the freedom that Christ bought for us with His blood.

God Has Given Me Victory

Come and be free. God gives you victory when you raise the white flag of surrender to Him.

> *"When you are about to go into battle, the priest shall come forward and address the army. ³He shall say: "Hear, Israel: Today you are going into battle against your enemies. Do not be fainthearted or afraid; do not panic or be terrified by them. ⁴For the LORD your God is the one who goes with you to fight for you against your enemies to give you victory."* (Deuteronomy 20:2-4)

Let's look at the situation described in the verse mentioned above. A battle is imminent. The army is amassed, and the priest/chaplain addresses the troops. For a Christian, this is an everyday situation. By a Christian, I mean a person who is a surrendered follower of Jesus Christ, not simply someone who owns that label as if it meant something, like I did for many years. True Christians go out each day as lambs in the midst of wolves. Our enemies are not the people who seem to cause us so many problems and heartaches.

No, rather it as Ephesians 6:12 tells us:

> *"Our enemies are not flesh and blood, but the rulers, the authorities, the powers of this dark world, and the spiritual forces of evil in the heavenly realms."*

We can't see these opponents with the naked eye, but we can see the damage they do as they steal, kill, and destroy the beautiful creations that God has given us.

If we could see our enemies with the natural eye, we would most likely turn tail and make haste in the opposite direction. But, instead, we are encouraged to not:

- Be fainthearted or afraid

- Be terrified

- Give way to panic

You and I know these three items describe how we often *feel* as we face insurmountable obstacles, difficult people, and frustrating circumstances, let alone catastrophic situations. Even though we might have such feelings, the appeal is to not give way (yield, surrender) to them. Our surrender needs to be in the direction of the One who alone fights for us against our enemies and gives us victory.

Instead of fixing our minds on the raging feelings inside, we can focus our faith on these unseen realities:

1. The Lord, our God, is with us,

2. To fight for us against our enemies, and

3. To give us victory

Note who does the fighting? And how do we get the victory? It is handed to us, placed right into our hands.

I faced numerous battles as a new follower of Jesus. For some reason, as a new mother faced with thinking of someone whose needs were totally dependent on me for much of the day and night, anger spilled out of my being. And this anger wasn't just limited to certain moments of weakness.

Before I had children, I thought I was a nice person. The constant demands of my children showed me a side of myself (I would call it the sinful side) that I had not been fully aware of. My firstborn son was nearly two before I recognized my sin, confessed it, and surrendered to Jesus. Amazingly, after that, I found my new Savior identifying battlegrounds where He would give me victory. My angry outbursts were the first to go. He fought this battle with me gently by showing me in His word, the Bible, and illuminating my perspective on anger.

First, Jesus revealed in James 1:20 that *"the anger of man does not bring about what is right before God."* (EHV) This verse stopped me short in my tracks because I wanted to do what was right before God but did not know how to. Surprisingly, the verse before it had the answer, *"My dear brothers and sisters, take note of this: Everyone should be quick to listen, slow to speak and slow to become angry because…"* (v.19)

Very gently (My dear…), God instructed me to reverse how I spoke. Instead of being quick to speak in anger and slow to listen, He encouraged me to be quick to listen (hear the other, truly listen), slow to speak (weigh my words), and, by then, anger would usually be dissipated.

God greatly encouraged me with another verse in those early days of following Jesus. As a new believer, I was painfully aware of how far I was from the holy life that God wanted me to live. He gave me a word that was originally given to the Jews who were coming into the Promised Land, Israel.

> *"I will send my terror ahead of you and throw into confusion every nation you encounter. I will make all your enemies turn their backs and run. ²⁸I will send the hornet ahead of you to drive the Hivites, Canaanites and Hittites out of your way. ²⁹But I will not drive them out in a single year, because the land would become desolate and the wild animals too numerous for you."*
> (Exodus 23:27-29)

You might be saying, 'What does that even mean and how was that encouraging?'

I understood from this passage that God was in charge of determining what enemies needed to be driven from my life, and He was in charge of the timing. It would be gradual so that the place they had occupied in my life could now be filled with God's Spirit.

Dear One, speak to your turbulent emotions right now. Say, *"Peace, be still. My God is with me. He will fight for me to give me victory in this situation.*

COME AND PRAY

Lord God, You are the Almighty One, the only One who can subdue the enemies that originate the darkness in this world. Yet, you call me to co-labor with you in the process.

I yield the fight to You and praise You for fighting for me and giving me victory over fear. Thank you for being in control of the process of driving out my enemies and filling me with your Spirit so that I can safely occupy the ground they formerly held. You are now Lord!

Do It Afraid

Come and be free. Understand that sometimes God may call you to do fearful work. Instead of backing away, draw on God's strength and do the work afraid.

Even though the people were afraid of the local residents, they rebuilt the altar at its old site. Then they began to sacrifice burnt offerings on the altar to the Lord each morning and evening. (Ezra 3:3)

In the verse above, the scene is set in the city of Jerusalem, a place still greatly devastated from the Babylonian ransacking and burning that occurred over 70 years prior. In the city was a mixed group of Jewish remnants from the northern kingdom of Israel who had migrated along with transplants from several countries formerly sent by Esarhaddon, king of Assyria. In addition to this mixed multitude were the exiled Jews who King Cyrus of Persia had returned to rebuild their temple.

Cyrus commissioned the Jews and granted them all the supplies they needed. Considering this, the question naturally arises: why *would they fear the local people?* These Jews are returning to reclaim ancestral properties so they and their families can resettle in Jerusalem and restore their temple. For the mixed multitude that had settled there during the Babylonian captivity (a time when most Jews had been taken captive to Babylon by King Nebuchadnezzar), the returning Jews brought with them fear and anxiety since the people feared that they would not allow them to participate in the rebuilding process.

To show their displeasure, the "squatters" hired counselors (lawyers) to work against the returning Jews and to distort and manipulate their plans. Opposition continued through the reigns of

Cyrus and Artaxerxes, falsely claiming that these Jews were rebellious and refused to pay the required tribute (tax). In response, Artaxerxes issued an order to stop the work.

You may find yourself in a similar situation. You have begun a specific work, but you are arousing opposition on all sides by completing it. You are being reported to the authorities, and multiple lawsuits are being leveled against you. Nevertheless, you keep continuing onwards. You are doing the work you feel God has called you to do and trusting in His deliverance.

Speaking from personal experience, I saw this happen to a ministry in our area that had been operating for some thirty years. During these thirty years, the ministry spread light and brightness in the world, doing God's work and aiding families and schools. Another ministry sued them because the name of their ministry included two words that were also part of the suing ministry. It seems the claim was that the local ministry was copying the other name, even though both names were unique, except for those two identical words.

Looking at the dilemma as an outsider, I thought the whole claim was ridiculous and out of character for how the Bible calls us to behave toward one another in the church. Consider the following verse:

"Even to have such lawsuits with one another is a defeat for you.
Why not just accept the injustice and leave it at that?
Why not let yourselves be cheated?" (1 Corinthians 6:7)

Amid the wrongful suit, the local ministry continued on with its work. In the end, the lawsuit was resolved, and they went on spreading light and goodness in the world, as they always had.

All the while, these faithful ministers trusted God's word in Psalm 18:35-36,

"You have given me your shield of victory. Your right hand supports me; your help has made me great. 36 You have made a wide path for my feet to keep them from slipping."

This anecdote exemplifies that we can put our trust in our God even when our livelihood or life is threatened.

With that said, perhaps one of the most dramatic stories of someone "doing the right thing afraid" is this story from The Huffington Post, February 25, 2013.

In 2005, a man named Brian Nichols—on trial for rape—escaped an Atlanta courthouse and, after murdering four people, forced his way into single mother Ashley Smith's home and held her hostage for seven hours. Ashley defused the situation by reading Pastor Rick Warren's best-selling book "The Purpose Driven Life http://purposedriven. com/" to Nichols, and the wanted man eventually surrendered to the police. (He's now serving multiple life sentences without parole.) Smith talks about how Warren's book changed her life.

"At that time in my life, I was really down in the dumps, and that was a life-changing experience for me because truly, of all the people that had a role in that day, of all the people that could have lost their lives, I was the one that probably should have," she says. "And instead of me losing my life—here I was the lonely, widowed, drug-addict mom who deserved death—but God gave me a brand-new life, one that I could never, ever imagine, as a result of just giving my life to Him. And through that, I've tried to do better since then."

This passage begins with the building of an altar. *What about the altar in your heart?* Is it in good repair, used daily as a place to offer thanks and praise to the God who is your shield of victory, the One who has made a wide path for your feet to keep them from slipping? Or, have you been so involved in worldly pursuits that you have neglected time and even thought to worship the living God who dwells within you?

Even though Ashley Smith considered herself a drug-addicted mom, she had spent time hearing from God through Rick Warren's book that morning.

If God has called you to do something that causes fear in your heart, perhaps forgiving someone who greatly wounded you or confronting someone who has violated your boundaries, do it. Maybe you have been called to serve a problematic group of people, and you feel inadequate, do it with fear brimming inside of you, just like the people in today's story. In the end, it was discovered that King Cyrus had commissioned these people for that work, and King Darius sent the following words to those opposing it:

"Do not disturb the construction of the Temple of God. Let it be rebuilt on its original site, and do not hinder the governor of Judah and the elders of the Jews in their work. Moreover, I hereby decree that you are to help these elders of the Jews as they rebuild this Temple of God. You must pay the full construction costs, without delay, from my taxes collected in the province west of the Euphrates River so that the work will not be interrupted." (Ezra 6:7-8)

COME AND PRAY

Lord God, I humble myself before You. I want nothing less than to continue the work You have given me, whether it is being a loyal spouse, a responsible parent, a faithful employee, or a ministry leader.

I commit to keeping the altar of my heart in good repair, coming daily to You in worship and seeking You in Your word. Knowing that Your perfect love casts out all fear, I bring my fears to You. Your love has been shed abroad in my heart by the Holy Spirit. There is no room for fear.

God's Ways Lead to Freedom

Come and be free by acknowledging that only God offers a peace that passes understanding. It is a peace that the world cannot give. Without peace, there is no true freedom. The shepherd, the king, and the sinner, David discovered true freedom by surrendering his life to God. This chapter has many verses from his Psalm 18, revealing the intimate relationship he enjoyed with the God who set him free.

¹⁶He rescued me from the mighty waters and drew me to himself!

¹⁷Even though I was helpless in the hands of my hateful, strong enemy, you were good to deliver me.

¹⁸When I was at my weakest, my enemies attacked – but the Lord held on to me.

¹⁹His love broke open the way, and he brought me into a beautiful, broad place. He rescued me because his delight is in me! (Psalm 18)

Dear One,

If you have followed all the way to this point, you know that the true God, the living God, the God of the Bible works from a place of love. His loving kindness leads us to repentance (to agree about our sin and to turn from it.) These verses from Psalm 18 reveal God's powerfully loving heart, the only love that can cast out fear. If you have decided to surrender your life to God's Son, Jesus, then the words of this Psalm apply to you.

You have probably heard the statement, '*We are all God's children.*' Some of the scriptures in the previous chapters have proven that statement to be false. We are all God's creatures, made in His image and likeness. But we don't become His children until we surrender to His son, putting our faith in Jesus for our salvation.

John 1 talks about the fact that God's own people, the Jews, did not accept Jesus.

"12Yet to all who did receive him, to those who believed in his name, he gave the right to become children of God—13children born not of natural descent, nor of human decision or a husband's will, but born of God."

When you believed in Jesus and trusted Him for your eternal salvation, God gave you the right to become His child.

I rejoice with you if you have made that decision because of seeing who God truly is, coming to know Him for yourself, and choosing to follow Him; then, you can enjoy the freedom He gives you to worship Him, to live without fear and anxiety.

"Also, we have seen for ourselves and continue to state openly that the Father sent his Son as Savior of the world. Everyone who confesses that Jesus is God's Son participates continuously in an intimate relationship with God. We know it so well, we have embraced it heart and soul, this love that comes from God.

17-18 God is love. When we take up permanent residence in a life of love, we live in God and God lives in us. This way, love has the run of the house, becomes at home and mature in us, so that we're free of worry on Judgment Day—our standing in the world is identical with Christ's. There is no room in love for fear. Well-formed love banishes fear. Since fear is crippling, a fearful life—fear of death, fear of judgment—is one not yet fully formed in love."
(1 John 4:14-18 MSG)

As I write this book, I have been praying for you because I want you to experience the joy and freedom that can only come from total and complete surrender to Jesus Christ, trusting him for your salvation. I pray that what follows from King David's words in Psalm 18 will be your commitment. *GOD made my life complete when I placed all the pieces before Him… He gave me a fresh start. Now I am alert to GOD's ways; I do not take God for granted. Every day I review how He works; I try not to miss a trick. I feel put back together, and I am watching my step. GOD rewrote the text of my life when I opened the book of my heart to His eyes.* (v.20-24 the Message)

You save the humble but bring low those whose eyes are haughty.

28 You, LORD, keep my lamp burning;

my God turns my darkness into light.

29 With your help I can advance against a troop[a];

with my God I can scale a wall.

30 As for God, his way is perfect:

The LORD's word is flawless;

he shields all who take refuge in him.

31 For who is God besides the LORD?

And who is the Rock except our God?

32 It is God who arms me with strength

and keeps my way secure.

33 He makes my feet like the feet of a deer;

he causes me to stand on the heights.

34 He trains my hands for battle;

my arms can bend a bow of bronze.

35 You make your saving help my shield,

and your right hand sustains me;

your help has made me great.

36 You provide a broad path for my feet,

so that my ankles do not give way.

37 I pursued my enemies and overtook them;

I did not turn back till they were destroyed.

(Psalm 18:27-37 NIV)

COME AND PRAY

Heavenly Father, I come before you on behalf of those who are reading this book. I pray that they have come to see that you are more loving and compassionate than they ever thought and that they know of your goodness through your word and obedience to it.

I pray that many have chosen to follow Jesus and enjoy freedom in Him. For those,

I trust that your perfect love will cast fear from their lives, and as they bring every anxious thought to you with thanksgiving, your peace, which passes understanding, will guard their minds and hearts in Christ Jesus.

I pray for them the prayer of Paul the apostle to the Thessalonians in 5:23,

May God Himself, the God of Peace, sanctify you through and through. May your whole spirit, soul, and body be kept blameless at the coming of our Lord Jesus Christ with all His saints.

For those who have not yet chosen to surrender to you, Lord, I pray that you will enlighten the eyes of their understanding, remove the veil that blinds them to the truth, and set them free!

Resources

These are materials, apps, etc. that I believe you will find helpful in going forward. You will find many others as you continue following Jesus. Since music addresses the right brain, it can get your soul ready to receive what God has for you in His word.

Music available on YouTube:

All My Questions – Bethany Barnard + Amanda Cook

Be Alright – Dante Bowe + Amanda Cook

Break Down the Walls of All My Religion – Chris Jericho

Break Every Chain – Jesus Culture

Champion – Dante Bowe

Come Again – Elevation & Maverick City

Dancing on the Waves – Bethel

Fall Afresh – Jeremy Riddle

Faithful Still – Kings Porch

Fear Is Not My Future – Brandon Lake

Fierce – Jesus Culture

I Speak Jesus – Charity Gayle

I Will Not Fear – Elohim Shomri

Lion – Chris Brown and Brandon Lake

Make Room – Community Music

No Longer Slaves – Zach Williams

Whom Shall I Fear? – Chris Tomlin

Worthy of My Song – Phil Wickham

ONLINE STUDIES/MESSAGES through apps

Awaken – app – contains pertinent, relevant messages from the Bible from multiple speakers

First 5 – app – a daily devotional

Give Him 15 – app – online Bible study

The Chosen – app **The Chosen** is the free show that millions of people are viewing. It explores Jesus from the eyes of those who knew Him. Stream the multi-season series free from the app.

Books

The Believer's Authority, Kenneth E. Hagin (Amazon)

www.ingramcontent.com/pod-product-compliance
Lightning Source LLC
Chambersburg PA
CBHW051211120626
46547CB00013B/1300